BOUNDLESS: 2022

THE ANTHOLOGY OF THE
RIO GRANDE VALLEY
INTERNATIONAL POETRY FESTIVAL

FLOWERSONG
P R E S S

FlowerSong Press
McAllen, Texas 78501
Copyright © 2022 FlowerSong Press

ISBN: 978-1-953447-04-3
Library of Congress Number: 2022936492

Published by FlowerSong Press
in the United States of America.
www.flowersongpress.com

Set in Adobe Garamond Pro

Typeset by Priscilla Celina Suarez
Design by Edward Vidaurre
Cover art, "Colorful World" by Fouad Reda

NOTICE: SCHOOLS AND BUSINESSES
FlowerSong Press offers copies of this book at quantity discount with bulk
purchase for educational, business, or sales promotional use. For information,
please email the Publisher at info@flowersongpress.com.

BOUNDLESS: 2022

THE ANTHOLOGY OF THE
RIO GRANDE VALLEY
INTERNATIONAL POETRY FESTIVAL

FLOWERSONG
PRESS

Selected & Edited by

**Gina Duran, Gabriel González Núñez,
& Edward Vidaurre**

Rio Grande Valley
International Poetry Festival
www.valleypoetryfest.org

Boundless is the official anthology of the Rio Grande Valley
International Poetry Festival (VIPF), founded in 2008 by
Daniel García Ordaz and Brenda Nettles Riojas.
VIPF is held annually the last weekend in April in deep
South Texas as a celebration of National Poetry
Month. Directed by Edward Vidaurre.

Contents

I.
SELECTED AND EDITED POEMS
BY GINA DURAN

II.
FROM OUR EDITORS

III.
FEATURED POETS

IV.
POEMAS SELECCIONADOS Y EDITADOS POR GABRIEL GONZÁLEZ NÚÑEZ

V. BOUNDLESS-YOUTH
POEMS & ART SELECTED & EDITED
BY EDWARD VIDAURRE

INTRODUCTION

In a world where many feel bound by constraints and restraints of systems of oppression, where words are used to seduce and instill fear and false hopes, we seek a world without borders— we seek to be *Boundless*.

2020 birthed 2021 and 2022, where Black Lives still seek to matter after hundreds of protests around the world. Where the lives of the marginalized fiercely grasp out towards the stars in refusal to be inundated and silenced. Refugees continue to migrate towards the countries that have caused their poverty, the dying go silently like nebulas without helium—but we still remember. People call out through prayer and poetry, to speak the vibrations of truth and find the echo of justice.

In this collection of poetry, we hear the whispers and sizzles of the sun rising in its glorious and tumultuous splendor. It is—at times—reminiscent of the Romantic, as it rapidly sets in the glow of rebellion and disillusionment with death and heartbreak. We witness the stories of our ghosts and those who are haunted. Some of those ghosts are our loves, some are our own despair, and others are our disease. We show that when sometimes anything is forgotten it is often not by choice, but from the pain of lost memories while our loved ones hold us in their hearts. We see that sometimes we forget who we are, but that it is often our loved ones who remember us in the fragments of things. Yet, we continue to build and look for the answers. We continue to thrive and dream and dance and sometimes it is in denial and sometimes it is in truth, but no matter what there is still love buried deep within as we live out simultaneous realities and often shared experiences. There is love touching the lips of the foraged morning dew on a leaf. There is love in the rebellious strife for survival. And there is love as we take our first and last breaths.

We have the chance to read the stories of those who wake and do not wake in poetry. We have a chance to see the mundane and the extraordinary all at once. We see moments and years pressed into seconds, as though we are the creators of this world—because we are.

I hope you have the chance to see the people around the world, who tell and retell stories in this collection. Then sit and watch the sun set and rise, as we begin again—with *Boundless 2022*.

— Gina Duran, Editor

INTRODUCCIÓN

En un mundo en el cual muchos se sienten atados por las limitaciones y restricciones que les imponen unos sistemas de opresión donde las palabras se usan para seducir e infundir miedo y crear falsas esperanzas, nosotros procuramos un mundo sin fronteras, procuramos no tener límites, o como se dice en inglés, procuramos ser *Boundless*.

El año 2020 engendró al 2021, y éste, al 2022, donde las Vidas Negras todavía buscan importar después de cientos de protestas por todo el mundo, donde las vidas de los marginados dan manotazos intensos hacia los cielos negándose a ser vencidos y silenciados. Los refugiados siguen migrando hacia los países que han causado su pobreza, los moribundos se mueven en silencio cual nebulosas sin helio, y aun así, recordamos. La gente llama por medio de la oración y la poesía, para enunciar las vibraciones de la verdad y hallar el eco de la justicia.

En esta colección de poesía, escuchamos los susurros y chisporroteos del sol naciente en su refulgencia de gloria y tumulto. Supone, a veces, una evocación del Romántico, ya que dicho sol rápidamente se pone en el resplandor de la rebelión y la desilusión ante la muerte, ante la angustia. Somos testigos de las historias de nuestros fantasmas y de aquellos que están embrujados. Algunos de esos fantasmas son nuestros amores; algunos, nuestra propia desesperación; otros, nuestras enfermedades. Demostramos así que si a veces algo se olvida, no suele serlo por elección sino por el dolor de los recuerdos perdidos mientras nuestros seres queridos nos guardan en sus corazones. Vemos que a veces olvidamos quiénes somos, y sin embargo con frecuencia son nuestros seres queridos quienes nos recuerdan en los fragmentos de las cosas. Sin embargo, seguimos edificando y buscando respuestas. Seguimos prosperando, soñando y danzando, a veces en negación y a veces en verdad, pero ante todo, lo que aún llevamos muy en nuestro interior es amor, amor en nuestras vidas de realidades simultáneas y también, con frecuencia, de experiencias compartidas. Es amor lo que se posa en los labios del rocío mañanero que se acumula sobre una hoja. Es amor lo que hay en la lucha rebelde por sobrevivir. Y es amor lo que hallamos en nuestro primer y último suspiro.

Tenemos la oportunidad de leer los relatos de quienes saben despertar con o sin poesía. Tenemos la oportunidad de ver lo mundano y lo extraordinario a la misma vez. Vemos momentos y años comprimidos en segundos, como si fuésemos los creadores de este mundo, porque de hecho lo somos.

Espero que tenga usted, estimado lector, la oportunidad de ver en esta antología a las personas de todo el mundo que cuentan y vuelven a contar sus historias. Luego, le invitamos a sentarse y observar cómo se pone y sale el sol, mientras comenzamos de nuevo, con *Boundless 2022*.

— **Gina Duran, editora**

IN HONOR OF:

Jan Seale. 2012 Texas State Poet Laureate, McAllen, Texas
Emmy Pérez, 2020 Texas Poet Laureate, McAllen, Texas
Victoria Lopez, 2022 City of McAllen Poet Laureate

IN MEMORIAM:

Dr. Gloria E. Anzaldúa
Jovita González
Dr. Américo Paredes
Rául R. Salinas
Trinidad Sánchez, Jr.
Roque Dalton
Amiri Baraka
Mona Sizer
Eugene "Gene" Novogrodsky
David Wagoner
Thomas Kinsella
S Ramesan
Robert Bly
Baktash Abtin
Elizabeth Martínez
Jean Breeze
bell hooks

ANTHROPOLOGY AS POST-HUMAN HUMANITIES: SOME ANGELS AND THOUGHTS

An essay by Gary Snyder

The term culture has been around a long time and has had two meanings: one referring to highly artistic and socially cultivated people and events; the other meaning, as in 2021"yogurt culture" a medium of growth and nutrients which is how it came to be used in the term "cultural anthropology. The British have the term "social anthropology" instead. The other branch is "physical anthropology."

Before entering college I had already developed an interest in wild nature and pre-contact forests, and the ways of Native American people and how they had managed to get along before the arrival of all these Occidental tools and technologies.

In the Reed humanities courses, while truly appreciating the chance to learn the whole story of Occidental civilization, 1 was also wondering about the prehistory that went before, and the people on the margins of the high civilizations who had always been living by vernacular' sets of skills. When I took a course on East Asian history from Dr. David French, 1 got a taste of anthropology and then went on to another course with him which was about cultural anthropology. I felt that it provided tools for filing out my larger human curiosity.

The concept of "culture" cuts across race, language, place, and distinctions of civilized or uncivilized equally. Like the term "watershed" it forces us to reexamine what we assume to be the boundaries of the terrain. Literature is also within culture and every culture whether having a writing system or not, has a body of literary lore-in song and story that in part provides the "narrative" of the society itself.

The interest in narrative as an indicator has become much more developed in recent years. I became particularly interested in language, linguistics, and literary/performative manifestations of culture from early on. At that time we did not have the term "ethnopoetics" which has proven to be a very useful if somewhat marginal discipline.

I deeply respect the intellectual legacy of Franz Boas who did fieldwork in the maritime Pacific Northwest, and taught for many years at Columbia. Among the fine scholars and researchers who carried his work forward were Alfred Kroeber, Ruth Bunzel, Ruth Benedict, Robert Lowie, John Swanton, and not exactly a Boasian but very powerful thinker, the anthropological linguist Edward Sapir, among many others. Dr. David French's degree was from Columbia.

Of the fellow anthropology students of my time in the late forties and early fifties, Dell Hymes was something of a mentor and went on to become "a real" anthropologist with a long and distinguished career. He died in 2009. I went to a semester of graduate studies in anthropological linguistics at Indiana University but then turned toward East Asia. So left Indiana and transferred to graduate school at Berkeley where I studied literary Chinese and contemporary Japanese.

By that time I had come to think of myself as a Buddhist. I told Ed Schafer, my first adviser at Berkeley, that if admitted into the East Asian program I would not go on a Ph.D track— I simply wanted to enlarge my education. Being short of students they accepted me. That wouldn't be likely today. The rich political and literary scene of the Bay Area was attractive, and so even as a graduate student I had a foot in the literary world of San Francisco. I ended up making friends with Alan Watts and Kenneth Rexroth and then a little later Allen Ginsberg and Jack Kerouac.

My older (GI Bill) Reed friend Philip Whalen moved to the Bay Area and became part of those circles as well. Many other friends from Reed were in the Bay Area in the early and mid 50s including Jim Hatch, Robert Greensfelder, Grover Sales, Bob Saxon and others. Some of these folks I'm still in touch with.

Activism? Many people do not realize that besides being a cultural anthropologist and linguist, Franz Boas was a physical anthropologist. He and a number of his students did exhaustive physical studies on race through the 20s. His findings on race--namely that though there were some small differences that could be identified none of them were significant--became the legalistic foundation for the civil rights movement. Boas is not well remembered today as the North American intelligentsia has become more enthralled with European linguistics and Cultural Studies than the somewhat drier and anti-theoretical work of the Americanists. But in the American South, there are places where Boas is still reviled as the man who developed the scientific arguments that led to the legal conclusions underwriting civil rights legislation. An article finally giving Boas his due in this matter appeared in The New Yorker for March 8, 2004.

Dell Hymes, who in later years wrote a groundbreaking book called *Reinventing Anthropology* was one who pointed out that where earlier researchers in Native American language and culture maintained their "professional distance" from the individuals and groups they studied, as the 60s and 70s marched on and the Native American movement began to flower, anthropologists were called on to do more than just study people. If they were going to live and work and drink and sing with them then they should figure out how to be of some contemporary help as well. Reed anthropology graduate Dr. Michael Mahar made his name with studies of the Untouchable Castes of India, and has kept up his connections with them through the decades in a variety of useful ways; he is very highly regarded by the caste leaders as well as having his own special niche in the anthropological world. Michael was one of my good friends from even before college we met at St. John's High out in northern Portland.

At the edge of the Reed circle one thinks of Ron Scollon and his Reed wife Dr. Suzanne Wong. Their final book on culture, language, and literature came out last spring - *This is What They Say* - a complete revision of Li Fanggui & Ron Scollon 1976, then titled *Francois Mandeville's Chipewyan stories*. It is out of the Chipewyan Athabaskan culture of the Yukon, but speaks to a global ethnopoetic cosmopolitanism as well. Suzy Wong Scollon, also a Linguist, was with him in the research of the 7os, and helped him finish the final version of the project before he died in Seattle on New Years day 2009.

Paul Radin many years ago made an argument that cultural anthropology should not be considered a social science but a branch of history. I never entirely agreed with that, and I do think there is a real place for anthropology as a true social science. But for my own purposes I see much of cultural anthropology as a needed enlargement of the humanities. The "humanities" field needs to be able to open its view, now, to the depth of prehistory and the range of skills and customs and institutions that are out there everywhere. Whatever insights are gained by that can surely help serve the purpose of reducing misunderstanding. Maybe limiting warfare a bit, maybe finding an ecological balance somehow, in tandem with insights from the biological sciences and in particular the social or "human" side of ecology.

I've never lost my curiosity about the specifics of Occidental culture and recently re-read Livy's History of Rome. I'm thinking these days about the similarities and differences between Roman and Chinese imperialism. My interest in East Asia-China, Korea, Japan, Taiwan and VietNam has not abated. Cultural Anthropology helps provide some of the factual basics for not considering the Tibetans simply a marginal and backward branch of Chinese culture, as the official Chinese line would have us think.

The great work that anthropology (or whatever it will morph into) has yet to do includes educating world populations simultaneously to their unity and their diversity, to appreciation for deep history, to the simultaneous sense of place as little watershed and sense of place as planetary, and appreciation of our own species as having a flashy and somewhat special role in the big ecosystem. And of course recognition of the fact that humans, homo, is just one twig on this enormous organic biological tree.

Is this the new work of the humanities? Post-humanities, pan-humanities? Time will tell. Poetry as a Survival Skill I had always taken it for granted, living on a small farm north of Seattle in a house with two books, that reading was an interesting entertainment. (The two books were the King James Bible, which my parents scorned, and a mysterious volume of Robert Browning poems) I started reading early (public library), and tried my hand at a little writing from a young age but not too seriously and with just a little encouragement from my mother.

In 1945, the summer I was 15, I did my first snow peak climb, Mt. St. Helens. The following year I was out climbing Mt. Hood with the Mazamas and soon other Northwest snow peaks followed and I joined the Mazamas. It was mountaineering that made me try poetry: I could find no prose mode for the particular qualities of climbing on snow and ice in the very early morning up to high and radically different environments. Not that I wrote very much about it-but it gave me a start. The poetic models must have been Whitman, and other high school poetry anthology regulars. I memorized some Shakespeare. Late in high school and still in my climbing days I also ran onto D.H. Lawrence's *Birds, Beasts and Flowers* at the Portland Public Library and started listening to folk songs there (with a listening room), in particular Leadbelly. So my early poetry was shaped by a romantic sensibility. Once at Reed I learned to look down on that, and became swept along in mid-20th century modernism with Yeats, Stevens, Eliot, Williams, and Pound as masters and models. But Robinson Jeffers -- also a West Coast person -- was very important and fellow Reed students Phil Whalen, Lew Welch, and I read Jeffers with special attention.

My poems of that era were clearly derivative of the modernist fashions of the times. Lew was very taken with W. C. Williams and that was a helpful push for me. Philip was a broad-ranging thinker and reader who referenced poetry of all times and places as he went. Lloyd Reynolds taught the creative writing class and I took it one semester-he also taught calligraphy and printing. Philip and Charlie Leong were accomplished calligraphers in Lloyd's tradition and though I never took a calligraphy course directly from Reynolds I got his teachings through them. Lloyd's love of William Blake was contagious to us all.

And I mustn't forget William Alderson. The effect of Alderson's 18th century literature course was significant and useful. Reading the 18th century poets, I realized that one could be sardonic, sarcastic, write parodies, be political, be witty and dry and it still might be called poetry. The Alderson course on the traditional English and Scottish ballads was greatly important and sent me back to Leadbelly and the Appalachian vernacular singers recorded by the Lomaxes. I learned how to strum a few chords on the guitar. Alderson told us how he had studied with Bertrand Bronson at Berkeley (author of The Ballad as Song) who had studied with George Lyman Kittredge who had studied with Francis James Child of the Child ballads. Those interests meshed well with what I picked up in my anthropology courses on oral literature and the huge preliterate, prehistory of poetry as song, and the oral tradition. G. I. Bill student Charlie Leong, a Chinese-American who was born and raised in Portland but who had studied some traditional East Asian crafts including seal-carving, gave me a further push toward Chinese language and poetry. Dr. David French introduced me to local ethnography and linguistics as well as basic East Asia. Dr. Stanley Moore was a perfect model of articulate and unapologetic intelligence. The scientific, historical, and literary materials that I explored for much of the rest of my life were all in place by the time I finished at Reed College. Plus, my own feckless assumptions of self-sufficiency and radical independence that were somewhat softened by the warm support of friendships. Those have lasted all these years.

As for poetry -- three or four years after graduation I renounced it, and burned a lot of the derivative modernist poems of the Reed era. Then the summer of 1955 I took a seasonal laborer job on a trail crew in the Yosemite backcountry, and weirdly found myself writing down some things I had to call poems. They became the foundations for my first book Riprap and another part of my life was launched though at the time I didn't know it.

Gary Snyder was born on May 8, 1930, in San Francisco.

He has published numerous books of poetry and prose, including *Danger on Peaks* (Counterpoint Press, 2005); *The Gary Snyder Reader* (1952-1998)

(1999); *Mountains and Rivers Without End* (1997); *No Nature: New and Selected Poems* (1993), which was a finalist for the National Book Award; *The Practice of the Wild* (1990); *Left Out in the Rain, New Poems 1947-1985*; *Axe Handles* (1983), for which he received an American Book Award; *Turtle Island* (1974), which won the Pulitzer Prize for poetry; *Regarding Wave* (1970); and *Myths & Texts* (1960).

Snyder has received an American Academy of Arts and Letters award, the Bollingen Prize, a Guggenheim Foundation fellowship, the Bess Hokin Prize and the Levinson Prize from Poetry, the Robert Kirsch Lifetime Achievement Award from the Los Angeles Times, the Ruth Lilly Poetry Prize, and the Shelley Memorial Award. Snyder was elected a Chancellor of the Academy of American Poets in 2003.

He was the recipient of the 2012 Wallace Stevens Award for lifetime achievement by the Academy of American Poets. He is a professor of English at the University of California, Davis.

SELECTED AND EDITED POEMS BY GINA DURAN

Papas

by Laura Seldner

Once I went with my husband and his father to a salvage yard
and they pulled and pried, father and son,
parts they needed the way his father used to
unearth potatoes from the ground.
He used to, his father, watch rain run in rivulets
through cobblestones on the street,
he used to watch the clouds pour like sea foam into the valley,
he used to cut barley and chochos, use his thick fingers,
dirt beneath the nails, to pry loose stalks and grain.
When we went to the salvage yard it had been twenty-three years
since he'd plunged his hands into the earth of his first breath
and after they'd finished we ate
seco de chivo at a Dominican restaurant nearby.
Qué rico que es el seco, he'd said. Back home, you know.
How good the seco is. It had been twenty-three years.
And now he shows his son how to pick car parts, loosen them without breaking,
gather them, use them, fix something that is broken
because here there is no land,
there are no potatoes.

Laura Seldner is an emerging writer and poet currently living on the East Coast. Originally from New Jersey, she is a graduate of the Latin American Studies program at Rutgers University. Her work appears in *Lunch Ticket* and *Space City Underground Magazine*.

20 into 21

by Trevor Wainwright (Trev the Road Poet)

This morning, no time for yawning,
Or standing in the cold shivering there's food parcels to be delivering
Take them out so folk don't go without, then back more to pack
Stored in my garage so a call for help can be heeded
They'll go where needed.
When this was done I chilled for the afternoon
For soon with good intent I'd another commitment
Last stint at the food bank for 2020, over the year we've helped plenty
Showing we care and when people needed help we were there
That's done I've given my best now time to rest
Home, chill, write listen to music and singing
Wondering what the New Year will be bringing
For better or worse I hope to be there to catch it in verse
Then New Year's Day dawned dull an grey
The street I looked upon to find yesterday's frost had gone
And the UK's left the EU a task that took long enough to do
But I'm hoping in 2021, I can once more enjoy the hot Texas sun
Or better than not going at all the beauty of Texas in the fall
Now I've sorted my emails, facebook posts too, one thing more to do
End this rhyme cos' now, it's coffee time
Written as we moved from 2020 into 2021 as things happened, we decided to store food parcels in our garages in case of any emergencies over the holiday period, I work at two food banks one which delivers for people that can't get out and are considered vulnerable we are on call 7 days a week, and the other is a weekly distribution where clients collect, those that are able, and yes I did go for coffee.

Trevor Wainwright, known as *Trev the Road Poet*, he has been a regular international guest poet since 2012. Popular in the schools and among fellow poets, one of the UK's most prolific traveling poets, with a love of poetry and sharing it. Stopped by covid he is determined to return one day.

Sacredness of Life

by Tom Murphy

Greed, money and guns.
They took what they could

              carry
bellies painfully empty already.
Some place had to be better.

              Estados
Unidos, el Norte, hermano y hermana.
What was another river to cross?

              Begging
all fourteen hundred miles of walk.
Chased by ICE. No

              money,
no food, no water. Ripped and
battered. Estados Unidos

              no
bueno. Hunkered under a mesquite, alone.
No God, no burning bush, no talking

              Snake.
Solo quiero una oportunidad.
Fathomless that in Estados

              Unidos
is greed

              money
guns

              and
lies.

Tom Murphy is the 2021-2022 Corpus Christi Poet Laureate and the *Langdon Review*'s 2022 Writer-In-Residence. Murphy's books: *Snake Woman Moon* (2021), *Pearl* (2020), *American History* (2017), co-edited *Stone Renga* (2017). tommurphywriter.com

AZTEC MARIGOLDS
by L.E. Flores

Aztec marigolds upon an altar,
Sugared sweet name of yours,
Called home.

Bread of the dead and beloved offers,
Until midnight gives way,
For my darling to roam.

Beauty in living in love and in death,
The fire we stoked,
Kept alive in my breath.

Tonight in the dark, I dance in the depths
Of your heart, in your arms,
'Cause our love never rests.

Aztec marigolds, wild like the flames,
Licking this delicate life,
Never tamed.

Like flowers that burn on prismatic plains,
Our limited nights,
Are never in vain.

At dawn, candlelight fades on the altar,
Saints of another world
Call you home.

Day of the dead, my spirit does falter,
Your sugared sweet name,
Engraved in stone.

L.E. Flores has been writing for over a decade—mostly screenplays and short stories—as a hobby to himself. Recent years have found him steeped and enthralled by poetry. He lives in Cameron County, Texas and is currently working on his first book, a collection of poems.

LILY OF THE VALLEY
by John Grey

Here, the bells ring silently,
despite the wind's best effort.

Even my fingertip,
that acclaimed campanologist,
swishes the flower
and yet makes no sound.

So lily's clang
I have to imagine.

It's like a butterfly
quoting Robert Frost
if you ever wish to know.

John Grey is an Australian poet, US resident, recently published in Sheepshead Review, Poetry Salzburg Review and Hollins Critic. Latest books, "Leaves On Pages" "Memory Outside The Head" and "Guest Of Myself" are available through Amazon. Work upcoming in Ellipsis, Blueline and International Poetry Review.

Ironpath
by W. D. Mainous II

there was fog the morning he left hospice care
my grandfather packed his old pick-up early
and prepared for the drive

he remembers his ancestors
those that made their last stand
and the small few that surrendered

he set out to honor their
courage in that dry
dangerous landscape

he will reach skeleton canyon late
and that will be where his path ends

grandfather wishes he was with those
starving and outgunned warriors —

though he was not there
he believes he is returning

the chiricahua are one

his belief is a gorgeous people
will rise from despair

grandfather it is a far far better embrace

W. D. Mainous II is a resident of Edinburg, TX. He works as a tutor and in healthcare. Mainous holds a bachelors in English and another in History. He has work published in Odes and Elegies, The Windward, Martin Lake, Voices de la Luna. He enjoys groundskeeping and poetry.

A Break from the Heat

by Margaret R. Sáraco

The sounds of chirping robins
and rustling leaves
pass through
open windows
no unnatural clatter

no groaning air conditioner
that interrupts sleep,
the sunlight paints
my blue walls indiscriminately
scattering shadows and highlights

a soft breeze lifts
white lace curtains
in an arpeggio billow here
billow there
unlike the swelter

from days and nights before
this cool July dawn
is a benevolent surprise
as a counterpoint to bad news,
anguish and torment

a single perfect morning
pushing back for a moment
and offering a reprieve
until the thump of the newspaper
tossed onto the front porch
brings reality back to the day

Margaret R. Sáraco is a poet and short story writer. Publications include *Paterson Literary Review, Lips, Ovunque Siamo, Exit 13, Peregrine Journal, The Path: A Literary Magazine, Home Planet News,* and *Red Fern Review.* Her poem, "The Unlocked Door," received an Honorable Mention in the 2020, Allen Ginsberg Poetry Contest.

The Furor of Wild Things

by Kathy Trenfield Raines

Their own tornadoes grant us peace.
They are not at peace.
They are more anxious than we.

Will a hawk tear me into edible portions?
A rat snake swallow me whole?
A bobcat sever my spine?
Can I procure enough rodents for my children and me?

A marauding raptor ripped my leg.
Can I still kill? Up my game?
Stuff up on carrion?
Rabbits and squirrels won't slacken their pace.

A dreadful grinding whirs below, and limbs topple into grass!
Our nest! Orphaned eggs tumble onto a roof!
We cry and cry, but our little feet can't lift them!
Then we depart. What's done is done.

Will I be a fortunate one who gets to mate?

A red-tailed hawk espies me, a human, far below,
Sprawled on the grass, eyeing her with my camera.
Wary, she soars a few yards, then alights on a different pole.

We find solace in the whirl of their presence.
But, unless we trail garbage or offer seeds,
Unless they find us amusing,
They find little in ours.

Kathy Trenfield Raines, a happily retired English teacher, has published poems and essays in *Boundless, Interstice, Escuchame, Voices From the Chicho* and *Along the River 2,* and *Odes and Elegies.* She currently writes a monthly column for Port Isabel/South Padre Press's *Parade* insert, each featuring a different creature from the Rio Grande Valley.

Darkest Before Dawn

by Bruce McRae

Doped moon in the dregs of summer,
the vernal and venal delicately balance,
starlight sashaying homeward
in the roundabout void, the abyss collapsing,
God's darkness and Man's lights clashing,
forgivable slights and sleight-of-hand
all part of the show, all one with the plan.

Up at two a.m. with a heart ajar
after a heavy meal and sparring
bout with demon alcohol.
Running low on time to burn
while fiddling like a grasshopper,
noncompliant to the ant's complaint,
autumn in the green room stretching,
limbering up its vocal cords,
preparing to make a sweeping entrance.

On with the lamp, then off, then on again;
insomnia a kinder word than torment.
Contemplating opiates, turning pages
in every book on the bedside stand,
moonlight sliding into the never-never,
past mistakes bounding into future acts,
sleep abandoning its post, birdsong rising
and I've counted every ewe and ram,
disgruntled grumblings of the first ferry's engines
carrying out over the water.

Bruce McRae, a Canadian musician, is a multiple Pushcart nominee
with poems published in hundreds of magazines such as Poetry, Rattle
and the North American Review. His books are 'The So-Called Sonnets
(Silenced Press); 'An Unbecoming Fit Of Frenzy; (Cawing Crow Press)
and 'Like As If" (Pski's Porch), Hearsay (The Poet's Haven).

Shoebox of Memories

by Susan Beall Summers

a balmy summer gloaming
with the downy feel of thic humidity
twigs and leaves nurture an intentional flame
smoke rises as damp tender hisses

low clouds paint a pastel tapestry
of an acolyte announcing
Mars—rising red
with his cold, distant censure

flames fuel eccentric shadows
to dance a rhythm of the past
the night deepens
dove and crow long retired
owls awaken to curse mouse

the wild salvia clusters
still wet with afternoon raindrops
reflect the fire's glow
casts diamond sparkle
for an absent wedding band

Inside the house,
from the dark recesses
of a closet
a shoebox
—trove of lost love:
ticket stubs from a concert,
postcards from Savannah,
smiling faces at Christmastime when we were a family.

unopened, the box is thrust
into the fire
Mars approves.

Susan Beall Summers (Palacios, TX) has served on the board for Austin International Poetry Festival, hosted Texas Nafas poetry show on Channel Austin, and has been a featured poet at events across America. Publishing credits include Ilya's Honey, Di-Verse-City, Boundless, Heroine Chic, Crab Fat, Cattails, Frog Pond, etc. She has a full length collection and chapbook.

And Did She Not Say
by Ken Hada

how she loved summer night
falling, when the heat of day
finally cooled to 84, and humid
dark glimmered with fireflies,
southern breeze whispering
through the grass?

And did she not say how she
loves – needs – to hear crickets speak?
Can voices of childhood,
so easily forgotten, remind us
of desire – even clumsy rhythms
for which we yearn?

Ken Hada's two most recent poetry collections are *Contour Feathers* (Turning Plow Press, 2021) and *Sunlight & Cedar* (Vacpoetry, 2020). Ken's work has been awarded by the National Western Heritage Museum, SCMLA and The Western Writers of America. More at: kenhada.org

Deluge

by Jen Yáñez-Alaniz

We escape the night of our homes
the softness where we dream with our spouses the perfect constructs of our offspring
we gaze beyond the pink moon
into her shadows
hidden spaces where we once touched without boundaries of skin or restrictions
inflicted by
marrow and bone
we didn't expect to drown
our mouths open to the darkness
submerging our bodies
tongues unable to lap the deluge
the floods in our throats

Jen Yáñez-Alaniz is a Texas poet. Her work, Matrilineal Poetics: Toward an Understanding of Corporeality and Identity is featured in Latinas in Hollywood Herstories. Her latest and forthcoming publications are included in The Journal of Latina Critical Feminism, Cutthroat: Puro Chicanx Writers of the 21st Century, Rogue Agent Journal, the Mom Egg Review, and more. She is a Pushcart Poetry Prize nominee.

Star-Crossed

by Karen Cline-Tardiff

He fell from stars
      Didn't understand similes, metaphors
      Couldn't relate one thing to another

Astral conversations,
      star dust surrounding his verbs, adjectives

He spoke of galaxies
      We only understood our small patch of Earth
      Couldn't levitate
      Wouldn't be bothered to hear stories
         about planetary alignment, quarks

Sadness overtook him
      He tried to enlighten us
      Bring us into the future

Our obstinance, our ignorance, insurmountable

He left for the stars

We told stories about how he
      moved to Michigan, Texas,
      somewhere far away, but only as
         far as we could fathom

No one realized she was searching the skies,
      trying to catch a glimpse of him
      practicing levitation and astral projection
         alone in her room at night,
      windows open to glimpse the stars

Karen Cline-Tardiff has been writing as long as she could hold a pen. Her works have appeared in several different anthologies and journals, online and in print. She founded the Aransas County Poetry Society. She is Editor-in-Chief of Gnashing Teeth Publishing. When she can't find poetry somewhere, she puts it there.

borderland suburbia

by Kim Denning

Desert covered in deepest blue
in shadow of a mountain that threw no shade where houses grew out of sand
and lawns forced their way through the grains and foreign trees rooted tearing
out the creosote, lifting fauna into stones   on that side of the freeway
Where middle class lightened skin
tangling Spanish tongues
washing color down slopes of beige plateau   toward green line of the Rio
Things of this place, the "heights", the "woods" they pulled at my mother, pinching
threatening to rip her further from her Brown   in this painting of a place of sun
where darkness fades by de facto
and children must be either or   Because the plateau was a mesa—
a god damned Norman Rockwell of abundance on the table of Americana inventions
half-priced bargains in a fakery of choice   Until divorces came and
rent signs appeared and choice became heartbreak,
yards browning in sun, reclaiming to sand   grit devouring the mortars
of our crumbling walls that swept away
in flashes of flood and rising heat   and sliding breeze

Kim Denning is a Latina poet who prefers guitars loud with distortion. Her publications include *Last Stanza Poetry Journal, FERAL, OpenDoor Magazine, Pareidolia Literary, Boundless Anthology, Adanna Literary Journal's Women in Politics* edition, Versification, and soon- *Essential Voices: A COVID-19 Anthology.* She murdered romance by winning *Versification Zine's* 2021 Kill Cupid contest.

Life With Birds
for Javier
   by Chuck Taylor

When it gets cold I take the bus,
but when it's warm I walk
the long way home from school
whistling to birds in the trees,
not worrying what my nosy neighbors think
since they are at their jobs

No one walks the sidewalks anymore,
they all drive in cars.
I know the names of many birds
and know that all the birds
sing back to me.
We make a kind of holy congregation.

Am I the only man who sings to them?
I whistle clear the song of birds
and my humble trills make them happy.
I forget the parental dramas of my home
and the hormonal dramas of my high school.

Later I peer into the yard
and find it full of boat-tail grackles
flapping around for things to eat.
They gather the thickest after a rain
and pass on singing, these birds,
taking breaks on the fence

or up in the trees. They fly in from
a small lake a half-mile down the road.
I am sad when I see no other birds.
It makes me worried.
I hustle birdseed every day
out to our hanging feeder.

A pair of swifts comes to nest each spring
on our front porch to raise their babies,
Two hatched this year.
I am pleased to share a life with birds.

Chuck Taylor won the Austin Book Award. His latest are *Being Beat* (2018*)* , and *I Tried To Be Free (2020)*, both published by Hercules Press. He worked in the Poets-in-the-Schools, served as CETA Poet-in-Residence of Salt Lake City, operated Austin's Paperbacks Plus, and was Creative Writing Coordinator at Texas A&M.

Meditation for Soqui

by D.M. Chávez-Solis

The work and play of songbirds that skit
and flit, generation after generation,
about my winter Texan yard searching
for food, for seeds from old blossoms
and tired weeds. Chirruping and singing,
at turns rapturous…their dance and song

remind me of the work in your garden
in the desert, remind me of your
laughter, of your playful
rugged spontaneity,
and of your creative enthusiasm
for creation's mysteries and surprises…

reminding me, as you often did,
how beautiful life is
whenever we meet the Beloved
in trees, or on the highway,
in sunlight through delicate etchings
in the plainest chapel windows.

We fell into the holy again, falling
in love with the sacred as if newly
--every time we greeted one another,
taking the arms of our ancestors
and of the Beloved together,
taking each other's hand.

D.M. Chávez-Solis is a science writer and technical editor creating con-
templative, environmental, and LGBTQ+ poetry primarily from the
"wild" of remote and/or inner-city places. Her poetry and fiction have
appeared in America, Half-Mystic, Hubbub, Pudding, and RE:AL. She
lives with her partner on the Central Coast of California.

Reliance
[After reading "The Red Wheelbarrow" by William Carlos Williams]
by Natalie Reid

So much depends upon
the mother's first song,
trembling its message
into her infant's heart.

So much depends upon
the forked maple tree,
sweet sap rising
in the crook of spring.

So much depends upon
the still gray owl,
eyes boring into mine
until great wings spread.

So much depends upon
my small Tuvan horse
cleaving belly-high foliage
near the Khakassian border.

Natalie Reid, author of *The Spiritual Alchemist: Working with the Voice of Your Soul*, has published poems and short fiction in *Another Chicago Magazine, eMerge, Knock, Natural Bridge, 13th Moon*, various anthologies, and others. She teaches writing in the mythological voice and workshops at the confluence of creativity and spirituality.

Fear of The Good Lord
by Vito del Valle

Everything my parents taught me was a lie
All the words they spoke to me were meant to condemn me
   to a life of suffering
So many summers, spent working in the fields
Walking the rows of sugar beets, made me a man
it showed me the truth of men
There was no choice for me only regret
What I, could have achieved
What I, could have seen
What I, could have done
Who I, could have loved
Fear of the good Lord kept me in line
   forever walking the rows
   forever knelt in the pew
   forever the diligent worker
Submissive and silent for
   fear of the good Lord
The prayers, the lessons, the lies
   my parents taught me left wounds
Wounds that never healed
and speak to me of things that could
have been

Vito del Valle is a middle-aged punk rock/metal musician out of Donna, Texas. Vito writes songs and poems for his cats and whoever else is willing to listen.

HUECO TANKS

by Renee Williams

Among the stones I long to be
my only friend in life, a tree
I'd need no other company
nor walls, nor roof, to shelter me.

The sky, my father overhead
once kissed the ground on which I tread
as he claimed Gaia's maidenhead
one primal scream escaped and fled.

Wind sends its whistling lullabies
on open-winged dragonflies
as sunset cues the moon to rise
stars burn like fires in my eyes.

Coyote howling on the plain
delights me with his love of game
one need not ask the other's name
coyote? me? one and the same.

Tall grasses many secrets keep
of large things, small things, things that creep
they're holding vespers while I sleep
but they and I, we do not speak.

When hell hath frozen, I once heard
good souls will migrate heavenward
but only fish could be so lured
by dreams of flying like a bird . . .

. . . how absurd.

Renee Williams began writing poetry at age 16. What started out as self-therapy morphed into the preferred medium for channeling people, places and things she's encountered in her nomadic life. She's been published in 'The Ink Spot' and 'ByLine Magazine', and enjoyed belonging to various local writing groups in Florida, Texas and New Mexico.

loquats on 126th
by Stephany Bravo

wild roots took over the chain-link fence /
on opposite ends of grass / the loquat tree / and its
yellow-orange suns / our small brown hands would pick / feel for
their sweetness / force two to three / within the gaps of the chain-link
fence / after all that nudging and pulling / the stars still soft and
whole / we delighted in exchange / imagined each other's tongues /
swell with joy. / far beyond said loquat tree / its grass / and the
chain-link fence / our bearers eyes / fermented suspect gazes /
mediated protection spells / over barred windows / for guests they
knew little of. / we made communion / braided hair ends /
through chain-links / learned ligas and flower barrettes / roots over
loquats. / when the streetlights dimmed / when our mothers called for
us / when cars came and went / when the mellow breeze lullabied
branches / when i waited for apá to return / i contemplated your home /
all those rose bushes outside / wondered if your mom ever plucked a
few / placed them in jars around your home / like an offering to la
virgencita. / those wondering evenings / greeted me after school / your
home's interior unearthed / no jars / a kitchen table / curating
synthetic flowers / a dresser's mirror
illuminating / the sun's reflection / onto a pink
training bike / that had once patiently waited / its
front
wheel pressed upon / a slowly rotting loquat /
spilling its juices / the flies feeding /
buzzing in menacing
laughter.

Stephany Bravo is a doctoral student at Michigan State University pursuing a dual degree in English and Chicano/Latino Studies. Stephany's writing appears in *Dryland: A Literary Journal Born in South Central Los Angeles* and *Kairos: A Journal of Rhetoric, Technology, and Pedagogy.* Her piece titled "¡Tamales, Tamales, Tamaleees!" won the HYPHENS Essay Prize.

Genesis

by Marcella Prokop

at the dinner table, my mom and aunt
speak of chunchullo and mondongo
guts stuffed and fried or cut to bits and boiled
primal cuts of offal, food of campesinos,
food of my people
mom tells me my abuelita
used to buy bottles of blood freshly drained
from warm cattle to cook with spices, onions
and whatever else was in the pantry
the clots became like meat
mom recalled, coming to life and sustaining it
from 15 on
the year I became woman,
the year of my quince
I have been disgusted by my own blood
heavy with clots and the expectation
of what it is to be female, Latina
and my mother's daughter
what I didn't realize
until I too became mother
is the process of congealing within
sheds half-lives
and leads to whole possibilities
my grandmother stood
at the stove ripe for more than 10 years
with the bodies of 13 babies
today I feel her inside my own
and can't help but spin my blood story,
grateful I've shed some of the expectations

Marcella Prokop is a Colombian writer who lives and teaches in the Midwest. Her work has appeared in print or online in *The Brooklyn Review*, *Ploughshares*, The *Christian Science Monitor*, The *Fourth River Online* and *PANK*, among others.

For the archaeologist Stephen Miller (Stefanos) who died recently

by Spartakos Anagnostaras

A summer day in ancient Nemea
I look the restored sanctuary of Zeus
empty of your presence, Stephen

I see your footsteps, Stefanos
in the excavated stadium waiting eagerly
for the Nemean lion and Hercules

A long time ago in Goshen in Indiana
you asked your father about the job
that you should choose when you grew up

'God gives life for a reason
When you will discover the purpose of your life
you will live a happy life', your father told you

That day at the fountain of Goshen,
Neptune with his trident
transformed your childlike imagination into a shovel

The athletes in the Nemean Games
reminded me that the smile on your face of your childhood
existed for a reason

For the same reason that Kallipateira violated the ban
and became the first woman
to watch her son competing in the Olympic Games

Spartakos Anagnostaras was born in Athens in Greece. He has studied violin in Athens Conservatoire. He lives in Bristol in England. His poetry approaches last minute decisions and feelings of modern people who have so many communication networks but very few opportunities to communicate.

Does an Hombre Have to Die to Speak to His Own Father?

by Adrian Ernesto Cepeda

Papi, I don't want to wait to tell you, por favor, please—
trim those eyelashes and those ear hairs, way too long
many years, that's how long I remember us being
estranged, I used to tell mis amigos we only spoke
every cuatro años, during la Copa Mundial, and
los elecciones presidential? I used to believe we
were so diferente, you always towering above,
overshadowing me. Now I realize you were mi guía
to protect me, not ground me. I know, lo sé, you
helped me harness my voice I found in la poesía.
Whenever I had doubts, you always encouraged me
to sigue tu propio camino, my own path I followed,
 even when I asked, who am I, an author, published?
Me dijo, own this, hijo. I listened, te oí, I did and now
con every libro, book, volume, chapbook, review, you
always gush Papi proud. I don't want to wait to tell you,
I am a poet because of you, Soy Poeta! No longer
eclipsando, even millones of miles away you are always
at the side of my stage. Seeing the spotlight glowing on
my presencia, did you know, you gave me the entusiasmo
gift of palabras? I learned to savor the art of reading
from you. I also, don't want to wait to decirte, you have
the best laugh, I miss the bolstering sound of joy radiating
around the room, when your cheeks are puffy rojo, riendo
red. En serio, Gracias por el regalo de mis palabras. And
every time I stutter behind the podium, microphone
I become, su hijo, the sun, yo soy Ernesto, recitando
I have the strength to stand, pararse derecho— soy
agradecido, abrazos, Papi, I more than listened—orejas
abiertos—su hijo siempre, lo escuché.

Adrian Ernesto Cepeda is the author of *Flashes & Verses... Becoming Attractions* from Unsolicited Press, *Between the Spine* from Picture Show Press and *La Belle Ajar & We Are the Ones Possessed* from CLASH Books and *Speaking con su Sombra* with Alegría Publishing. Adrian lives with his wife in Los Angeles with their adorably spoiled cat Woody Gold.

PRODUCTIVE REPETITION

by Rent Poet, Brian Sonia-Wallace

Turn the oven to 375 degrees.
         Take the stairs down, two at a time.
                  The cycle of coffee
with mom, crying with mom,
         moving the car for street sweeping,
                  the workout rotation: legs, chest,
back, breathing books & drinking it black &
         every haircut is a complete reinvention.
                  Every time you put on
your shoes, you will never re-enter
         the room
                  you just left.

         My old lover tells me I am building a ritual.
         I see him infrequently. I see him again.
My mom tells me she is useless.
         I tell her stop being mean to my mom.
                  The pit of my stomach tells me
everything I want to hear. It sings,
leaps, stretches out, the thinnest spiderweb
         across a chasm, the wail of egrets
                  taking flight, that kind of beauty
white streaked against the sky.

I read the same poem to my ex-lover
         that I read to my class, realize
                  it has my dead dad all over it.
There's no such thing as broken.
         My mom says, "the hole doesn't close
                  you just have to embroider around the edges."
Like beauty is the pain that we attend to.
         Like the only way to keep living.
                  is to practice
& get better.

Brian Sonia-Wallace is the author of The Poetry of Strangers ("full of optimism and wide-eyed wonder...he charms us" - The New York Times) and Poet Laureate of the City of West Hollywood, the latest in a string of unlikely poetic residencies ranging from Amtrak to the Mall of America. Brian has written poems for over 10,000 strangers based on their stories since 2012 and is an Academy of American Poets' 2021/23 Laureate Fellow. The motto of his custom poetry business, RENT Poet is, "everyone needs a poem." More at briansoniawallace.com

After the Dementia Diagnoses

by Eric Devaughnn

That slender break
up and through the corner of her lip, longer than
what we remember having known. Each new
unfolding of our days creased into curious
wrinkles: this is the way memories rest in our crevices.

Spreading of a mouth as wide as ponies prancing
loose, their light and bouncing hooves, the toothy tickle
we have become.

Upon the calendar's rote acknowledgement of mothers
we wake to find the cherry blossom sky streaked a heavenly
orange hue.

I've begun to notice a spent crackle around my eyes, a sweet
patina, the gentle spread of these last many years. We allow
our children to fumble and explore until they stumble
into art, without gifting ourselves the same grace.

Eric DeVaughnn is a father, author, educator, and poet. He has hosted open mics, facilitated workshops with the local literary laureate, and is cofounder of innateDIVINITYbooks. He has three self-published collections. A new title is forthcoming. Eric received two degrees in Kinesiology from California Baptist University. He teaches elementary physical education in San Bernardino, California, where he resides.

All his poems are cracked teeth, dusky yellow and receding gum line lying
limp on waxy, bright white paper, speckled red.

11-1

by Ed k Gonzales

Auspicious; conducive to success, it is a very accurate assessment of our mother
Like all great beings that plunged themselves in to inhospitable circumstances
not for fame or glory she would not ever do that and my grandstanding would
guarantee me "the Look" you never want that to happen as generally be the
first step and or steps toward my demise, unless I fly-right I assumed initially
everyone had a single parent who worked two jobs to keep her five children in
Catholic school and behaving properly but as time wore on my older siblings
took to follow her footsteps of how to live a proper householders life and doing
whatever needed to be done, with that said I sit here alone typing a elegy for
a person who at one point in my life was my world and how I came to it, as I
prepared for her services I found amazing aspects of a very astonishing person as
she was a graduate of a university all the while helping to raise her eleven siblings
of which she was the eldest, also working at the family store and kept bees for
the family then leaving Texas for Los Angeles to begin her married life so I began
to appreciate even more her greatness although these are not words she would
use to describe herself all the pieces coming together to give us preparation for
life beginning on such an auspicious date 11-11 also not surprising some of my
siblings also born on auspicious dates as well as I pass this new found wealth of
information about her to my children, now adults about their ancestor so they
may see where they came from so they may pass along to their progeny with that
Happy birthday Mom till we meet again

Ed k Gonzales was born in Los Angeles in the French hospital in the
middle of Chinatown next to stadium way (Go Dodgers). Gonzales went
to Sacred Heart school in Lincoln Heights then Salesian high in East
L.A. then found himself in Texas caring for his wife's parents in the hill
country. There befriended A.Keith Walters who introduced him to the
Sun Poet's Society.

Rematriation / Rematason

by Tezozomoc © 2021 05 27

"We support the full sovereign expression of all our Indigenous relatives and believe that it is through the process of Rematriation that we reclaim our identity, our culture and our ways. Much of our cultures are deeply rooted in our Earth Mother and celestially connected to the matrilineal, uterine lines of our families, our people and our nations that extend beyond this world." -- Rematriation.com

My father passed away back on Nov 8th, 2006. It was not a surprise nor a sudden event. He had been fragmenting in place for over 8 years in a Delano nursing home.

In 1998 he had been diagnosed with leukemia; cancer of the blood. He was a typical banal Mexican man from the ranchos, what they call a 'chero, from ranchero. He was driven by the materiality of his subjectivization.

He was a man prone to what, Josiah Luis Alderete, calls the "Chinga tu madre blues!", a default exclamation when buttressed by situational impotence. Typically, paired with the, "Si no me la puedo coger", failed proposition. During his chemo treatments he failed to take care of his latent diabetes and he suffered several strokes. The irony of the "Chinga tu madre blues", is that he survived and recovered from leukemia, but his totality had been shattered by the catastrophic strokes he had endured. He began to enter a long enduring fragmentary flow of mental health decomposition. There were the physical violent episodes where he broke doors and sheetrock walls.

My mother, weathered and worn, was a good soldier, but the war was bigger than her. Like a good Adelita, she refused to abandon the battlefield but conceded and we finally took him to a Delano hospice center.

It was a good clean facility recently built and my uncles lived within minutes of the facility and would visit him when my mother couldn't. Migrations are transgenerational traumatic events moving at different velocities and across multi-generational bodies of varying tensile strength. My grandfather came with the Bracero program of 1942; Mexican cheap labor to buttress the 2nd world war. He was the anchor pulling across the norteño narrative space. The suspended lives that needed to disconnect from the materiality of their bioregionalism. Más cariñosamente conocido como tu terruño.

The deterritorialization of ribosomal organelles ripping through endoplasmic reticulum and nuclear envelopes shattering the four strands of eukaryotes and prokaryotes rRNA. Unwinding my progenitor.

Today, my father is buried in Delano at the Northern Kern Cemetery District off Garces Hwy. It wasn't the one my mother had paid for; she had allocated two spots in the Forest Lawn Cemetery, even though there is no forest left, just a lawn with tombstones and mausoleums. His family wanted him there. But they forgot to pay and my mother bore that debt.

A small epitafio signaling, el reposo, the rematriation point, the re-wombing, the gestational maternal reclamation. At the interment hole we gathered as a sanguine collection of strewn DNA strands vibrating and rattling in an attempt to heal a wound.

The Catholic priest swung his golden ornate thurible with its myrrh incense, like a Foucauldian pendulum marking the start of reclamation. The priest began to voice the final Catholic Sign of the Cross Prayer, I heard in my mind, In the name of gravitational forces, in the name of weak nuclear forces, in the name of strong nuclear forces, in the name of electromagnetism.

Tezozomoc is a Los Angeles Chicano Poet and 2009 Oscar Nominated Activist and has been published by Floricanto Press, "Gashes!: Poems and Pain from the halls of injustice", a collection of poetry, ISBN-13: 978-1951088040, 9/2019. He has also been published in the following journals: The Oddball Magazine, 06/19/2019. Spitpoetzine, Volume 6, 6/15/2019. The Silver Stork, silverstorkmagazine.weebly.com/, 2018.

Deciduous

by Romaine Washington

green/gold leaves shimmy
in a lazy blue sky,
                        indifferent
branches giggle and gyrate
in breezy autumn
surrender.
my son calls them laughing trees
where time counts backwards,
bare-limbed.
this year
they fall faster
in a furious rain,
burying themselves and us.
too many to count
so many to mourn
when i turn on the news
100,000 - 250,000 – 500,000
a million plus
        casket the earth.
                        unearthed,
        we hostages
sheltering in place
                grieving.
grieving
        sheltering in place,
        we hostages
                        unearthed.
                casket the earth
a million plus
100,000 - 250,000 – 500,000
when i turn on the news
so many to mourn
        too many to count
burying themselves and us.
in a furious rain

they fall faster
this year.
bare-limbed
where time counts backwards
my son calls them laughing trees.
surrender
in breezy autumn
branches giggle and gyrate
                    indifferent
in a lazy blue sky
green/gold leaves shimmy

Romaine Washington M.Ed. is the author of the poetry collection, Purgatory Has an Address, (Bamboo Dart Press, 2021) nominated for a Pushcart Prize, and Sirens in Her Belly, (Jamii) BET Editor's Choice top ten must-reads for 2016. She has presented her poetry in venues such as the CATE Conference, National Poetry Slam, KPFK, and NPR.

Washington's poetry has also been nominated for Best of the Net and has appeared in local and national publications some of which are *California English Journal; Becoming a Teacher; The Black Scholar; New Directions: Howard University; Lullwater Review: Emory University; Gathering: A Women Who Submit Anthology; Hip Mama; and The Verdict Is In.*

The days and two years

by Joselin Mejia Garcia, Translated by Francisco Chávez Becerril

Chaos is a hiatus,
a ladder,
to discover the concealed order,
chaos is nothing but man.

Li Wenliang announcing SARVS:
Rome, Paris, New York confined;
the first, the second, the third wave.

Ecuador and the dead on the street,
Antigone, Polynices and Creon in 20 20;
a covid rave/fest, herd immunity.

Minneapolis in flames,
America for the Afro-Americans,
the attack on the Capitol, the trumpist
farewell.

6 paralyzed subway lines, the futuristic collapse,
the return to the vaccination age on a wheelchair,
dragging one's feet with more than 60 years on top,
12 states without electricity in a post-strident-ist, Zoom-ist era.

Chaos is the principle of order,
it separates, unifies, and sustains,
it balances that which is in the cosmos.

Joselin Mejía García (México, 1993). Her poems have been anthologized in the following publications: *Jardín de figuras abiertas II* (México, Bitácora de vuelo, 2021); *Laboratorio de letras, Volumen 2* (México, Capicúa, 2021); *Boundless 2021: The Anthology of the Rio Grande Valley International Poetry Festival* (Texas, USA, FlowerSong Press, 2021); and in *Lecturas pandémicas, reflexiones en tiempo de cuarentena, Vol. 2: Maya* (Chile, La Gata Press, 2021).

The Nightmare
by Mark Esperanza

The bull dug his horns deep against the night,
Spinning dead leaves into a marron-covered moon.
His grunts shook the earth.
His kicks threw black dust in circles
As he disappeared and reappeared
Into the revolving air
That twisted lights and shadows
Like dying embers
And a glow grew along the hooves.

The hooves pounded coal,
Raised a flame to a fire.
He lowered his head and his stout.
Ivory horns traced in red.
He flared his nostrils
And caught my glance.
Then he bullied the ground with his right leg
Maddening.

I turned around looking for a place run
But a fence encircled us.
He grunted and twisted and kicked and charged.
I rolled on my back
Held my knees to my chest.

Clash! Clash! Clash!
Against my bedroom wall!

I awoke to a nightmare image of my mom on a red floor.
And my father standing over,
Like thunder.

Mark Esperanza, an Edcouch-Elsa, Texas writer and poet, currently teaches high school in the US-Mexico borderland city of San Juan, Texas. His creative work appears in numerous anthologies such as Lamar Press' *Writing Texas* and *Boundless 2021: the official anthology of the Rio Grande Valley International Poetry Festival.* His most recent research on ELL students appears in *Imaginative Teaching through Creative Writing: A Guide for Secondary Classrooms.*

Tlacuache Lynchings

by M. Anthony Miranda

there was one discovered this morning
playing dead

pitch-forks, shovels, a bone-crushing cinder block, and
the rancor in their choices

this morning a tlacuache was discovered in the trash can

playing dead
empowering and dismissing all in one macabre calamity

artificial or otherwise

and all equally turn dead

and it's ok

if it's a tlacuache you kill

for all eyes dilate equally and the same

around here people warn you not to let the tlacuache bite you
after all, tlacuaches carry disease and rabies and God knows what

and not
or
they stress

and pitch-forks, and shovels, and the barbed-wire fences, and the check-points,
the traps, and the sensors, and the cages, and the patrol vehicles, and the fences

the walls

there was another one discovered this morning – yet again no one said a thing

elevated sainthood and dual monstrosity
in one sacred murder beyond the brush-line and the shadows and the fences of
our border towns

and all turn dead and no one says a word

M. Anthony Miranda was born in 1974 and was raised in what is
commonly known as the Mid-Valley. Much of his experiences growing
up in the border communities of South Texas inspire the depth of his
writing, choosing often to illustrate the effects of institutional structures
as they shape the traditionally marginalized and under-represented
border communities where Miranda resides.

Parking Lot Prayer

Inspired by people blowing the Shofar outside of a hospital for Covid patients.

by Michael Gerleman

The old ways are best
when you cry out to God
during times of famine
or pestilence.
The piled into trucks, radios
playing tejano or rock or rap
gathering like a lost tribe of
Israel in the hospital parking
lot, donning shawls and
vestments like they were
at the wailing wall. They
blew their shofars and
suddenly the parking lot was
a desert, a mountaintop, a cross
topped hill and the ageless,
endless dialog between God and man,
beseeching, supplicating,
begging, promising, hurling
prayers into an abyss of silence,
waiting for God to notice.

Michael Gerleman is a teacher in South Texas. He attended the University of Northern Iowa for his B.A. in English Education and earned his Masters in English Literature from the University of Texas at Brownsville. He loves the vibrant art scene of the Rio Grande Valley.

From that Time I Wanted to Trade My Soul
by Giana Hesterberg

trading my petite, wide feet, toes down in a row,
for their long, slender ones, middle toe out to party

my short, stout legs planted like mesquites
for their perfectly shaped calves

my imperfectly-spotted skin
for their flawless, porcelain-freckled epidermis

they can have my soft limbs
if they give me their muscled physiques

my hourglass figure for their bouncy,
thin waists and hips

my huaraches for their wooden shoes

my Sombrero Festival for their Klompen Classic

my Charro Days for their Tulip Time

my Brownsville dirt roads for their Pella cobblestone streets

my Mexican-American heart
for their Dutch fronts

my thick, course, curly hair
for their wispy, blonde locks
my Virgin Mary for their Reformation

my veiny, old lady hands
for their long fingers

my buñuelos for their poffertjes

my empanadas for their Dutch letters
my palm trees for their maples

my South Padre Island for their Lake Red Rock

my small, brown-skinned people
for their tall, Aryan ones

my ranchos for their farmlands

my Anita for their Virgie

my panaderias for their bakeries

my "I'm too Latina to consider"
for their DTRs (defining the relationship) on a park bench

and my vatos for their wasps

G.G. (Giana Gallardo) Hesterberg was born and raised in Brownsville, Texas. She published her first book, *Stories by the Seashore,* in March of 2019. Her second book, *Music, Music, You Can Too!,* a nonfiction children's book, was released in July 2020.

The following poem was inspired by a former migrant student of mine who was accepted by Harvard. He wanted to major in biomedical engineering because of his grandfather, Don Antonio, who could no longer walk because his knees were worn out due to the years of working in the fields:

Don Antonio Gonzalez
by Ralph Haskins Elizondo

At the age of ten he first prayed to Our Lady of the Fields,
long summers spent on his knees in prostrate prayer
looking down, and sometimes looking up
to keep the sweat from stinging his eyes,
praying to the onions and the strawberries,
to the watermelons and the cucumbers.
His hands still carry the calloused, stigmata scars
of the harvests. With his wife and children,
in their green Ford truck with the missing tail-light,
children on the bed, and running on holy water
sprinkled on the hood, he made his annual pilgrimage
to the blessed fields of the north
where the patrón always pays well.
They spent their summer nights under Nebraska's trees
or inside Michigan's barns; but he always answered
the daily dawn's call to prayer at twenty cents a bushel.
His family answered too. They prayed and earned together.
He no longer makes the annual pilgrimage.
It is not meant for old men.
On any given Sunday he gives thanks for his good life
at the shrine of the Virgen De San Juan Del Valle,
the patron saint of migrants. He sits beside his walker
in her presence. Forgive him if he doesn't kneel this time.
He left his knees behind down the decades of praying
In the blessed fields of the north.

Ralph Haskins Elizondo was born and raised in Monterrey, Mexico. His family moved to South Texas during the social turmoil of the 60's. The new cultural challenges he experienced led him to express himself through poetry. Many of his poems touch the cultural and political issues of our times. His works have appeared in Puhnk And Miscellany Magazine, The Best Unrequired Reading In American Literature 2011 (Harcourt), Poesía En Vuelo, La Bloga (Poets Responding To SB 1070), and Poetry Of Resistance Anthology. Today, Ralph lives in McAllen, Texas. He recently retired after 37 years of teaching.

Death Haunted by Humans

by Sharon Elliott

Death Bringer plays a melancholy waltz on a button accordion
says humans are an enigma in their ugliness and their beauty
a riddle with no reply

cloaked in thunder mystery seeps into bones
made of jellyfish and lead

everything is stuck behind clouds
waiting
live the years wisely with reckless abandon
take care not to be too careful

in the slow inexorable twisting of the spine
a dance emerges
graced by whispers in the red night
mumbles carry messages too still for ears to hear
unless attention is paid

give thanks for eyes with vision
blessed by spirits hiding clarity
showing faces in the carpet down the hall
that which is breathing contains the secret word
blown by closed lips into sacred union with stones

what is awaiting transition won't have to wait long
a split second rides the wind
catches the ferry
rests in the depths

Born and raised in Seattle and recently relocated to Albuquerque, **Sharon Elliott** has written since childhood. Four years in the Peace Corps in Nicaragua and Ecuador laid the foundation for her activism in multicultural women's issues.

The Tag That's Still There

by Linda Romero

The gift bag had your name tag
on it still:

> To: A
> From: Mary

It blended in with the huge
Santa that took up the size
of the bag, unnoticed
as this year's gift was pulled out -
Given for someone else,
With no new owner's name attached

Then the brainstorm began:
What did she give you that year?
The black leather bomber jacket
you wore almost daily?
Maybe the sweater or blue knit scarf?

I kept staring at the bag as I held it,
as if remembering would make you real again;
As if, remembering would bring back the scent
of your Old Spice cologne and you'd be sitting
on the couch with your fedora hat on your knee
and laughing at my silliness as Jazz
played on the turntable

Pulling the tag off gently would leave
no tears or sticky residue to harm it;
But I couldn't bear to remove it -
Thinking I would forget more of you
before next Christmas

And it's still there.

Linda Romero is from Harlingen, Texas, and has been published in the VIPF Boundless anthologies, Along the River 2: More Voices from the Rio Grande (VAO Publishing), Twenty: In Memoriam (El Zarape Press), and La Bloga. She was nominated for a Pushcart Prize in 2018 for her poem, "In the Passenger Seat" by El Zarape Press which appeared in Boundless 2017. She is a Certified Academic Language Therapist and has a private practice providing dyslexia therapy.

Consejo (Advice)
by Karina Flores

I miss her
We had a language barrier
And you can blame that on our education system that hammered in on English
Leaving Spanish by the wayside
I miss her, my abuela
I miss her, though we could barely communicate I spoke broken Spanish
Told her that I was doing okay in school
That I was doing okay at work
Todo va bien, I'd repeat over and over
Would recycle the same words hoping that they'd find new meaning
But despite the barrier
There was no wall between us
She was warm, inviting
Made sure to feed us, though we'd sometimes arrive with no appetite
But you ate because she cooked it with amor, and you better respect that
We'd spend all afternoon in her home, watching late night Spanish variety tv like
Sábado Gigante
While ama and her talked over the latest gossip of our family
I wish I could've have spoken to her
Learn about our story
And tell you about it, really tell you
Because I just know her story was fascinating
But she left,
before I could find the words
My piece of advice?
Find the words

Karina Flores received her MFA from UTRGV. Publications include, "Anxiety" published in The University of Oklahoma's *Blood and Thunder: Musings on the Art of Medicine*, and "La Magia Divina de Natalia: Un Homenaje a Natalia Lafourcade" published in *The Mixtape Literary Journal: Tumbao! Louder Than Borders Vol. 1* 2021.

Zelda's Ghost

by Lu Lynne Streeter

Rippling piano crescendo
Arrogant chinon tilts toward
The glassine mirror
Sleek black torso, dead white skin
Sensuous arms, ankles
Turned just so
Madame counts 1-2-3-4
Lips press together
Intent on jeté, plié, relevé
Old floor creaks
Summer in Montgomery
Air barely moves
The dancer breathes
Skin shines with effort
Long legs lift
Inside her mind
Winter in Paris
Bees buzz, ants crawl
A ballerina in a music box
She cannot stop
Lid always open
The spring unwinds
She falls and falls
And falls. . .

Lu Lynne Streeter is an award winning poet, author and journalist. She is a recipient of the Christina Sergevna Prize at the Austin International Poetry Festival, an Honorable Mention at the International Human Rights Contest, a juried poet at the Houston Poetry Festival and a Pushcart nominee. She lives in Fredericksburg, Texas.

Bomber Jacket

by Chara Booker

As a child, I would explore my grandparents' closets
Full of monkey-like curiosity
Breathing in my Grandmother's scent of
Gardenias remaining in her coats.

That was how I found the Bomber Jacket,
The brown leather worn with age,
The lining silky soft.
I slipped my arms into the sleeves,
Sliding over my hands,
To show my Grandfather.

He told me a story of his time working with the Air Force in WWII
"I got the jacket and a Colt pistol from them. I gave the gun back afterwards
But I wish I had kept it!
It would be worth a fortune today!"

I was happy to find the survival guide in a secret pocket
I read about how to make a monkey trap
And then I built one in the backyard
Because I wanted a new friend.
I was so disappointed
When I had an empty trap at day's end.

How shocked I was when my Grandfather told me,
"They trap the monkeys to eat them."

Chara Booker is a published poet who also writes in prose. She lives in San Antonio, TX with her dog, Max, and cat, Sylvie. Seeing the poetry in the rhythms of our days is an inspiration for Chara; writing was as important as breathing to her during the CoVid times.

JUMBO
by Clyde L. Borg

Jumbo, Jumbo, Jumbo,
Eleven and a half feet,
A railroad train
Ran Jumbo down.

Jumbo, Jumbo, Jumbo,
Six and a half tons,
Barnum's greatest prize,
A tragic loss.

Jumbo, Jumbo, Jumbo,
Only twenty-four,
Jumbo's huge carcass
Made the show.

Jumbo, Jumbo, Jumbo,
So immense
His name defines
Enormity

Clyde L. Borg is a retired high school teacher. He has been writing Poetry and nonfiction since 1998. Some of his work has appeared in History Magazine, Leaves Magazine and Fate Magazine. He resides in Fords, New Jersey.

金継ぎ
To Constance Plumley

by Robert Beveridge

The sun is awkward and leads us
to places of which we have no memory.
Better, then, to embrace the dark
that hides under the bushel, the sweet
aroma of loam, must, decay.

You spoke of the wolves at the door,
your need to make them feel welcome.
No one told you they feed just as well
on meat tenderized with chloral hydrate
as with bromelain. Predators
in slumber easily removed
with a dolly, a little elbow grease.

One last wolf has come to call; he wants
to eat you, yes, but works to prove
his worth by chopping onions, mending pots.
He touches you with care, his claws
held back on cobblestones,
devours you only with his eyes.

Robert Beveridge (he/him) makes noise (xterminal.bandcamp.com) and writes poetry in Akron, OH. Recent/upcoming appearances in The Sparrow's Trombone, The Deadlands, and Of Rust and Glass, among others.

Bluebonnet Whispers

by Stephen Schwei

Just this side
of a bluebonnet field,
the sun squints
through the pines
above a cluster
of smoke columns,
topping each plume
with a candle flame.
Pines dominate the land
where campers graze,
concealed in fabric shelters
from which whispers wisp
during the evening pause.
The grace of the day
folds into the hollow
dark of the night.
Mysteries unfurl,
furtive possibilities scamper.
Adventurers peer out,
forage, seeking revelry
in forest pockets
or quiet contemplation
by the campfire.
Planned connections
and happenstance
occurrences ignite
with sparking logs.
Embers linger,
explorers retreat,
as satisfied murmurs
behind the flaps
slink away until dawn.

Stephen Schwei is a Pushcart-nominated, published poet with Wisconsin roots, now living in Houston. A gay man with three grown children and four wonderful grandchildren, he can be a mass of contradictions. Poetry helps to sort all of this out. www.stephenschwei.com

Where Springtime Lingers
by Ann Howells

they gather in confused delight
pull light about their shoulders

weave white flowers in long hair
cheeks flushed like peonies

they roar instead of laugh
weep instead of cry

when they open their throats
white butterflies burst forth

they leave red lips on tulips
sweet scent on the breeze

part of nature like scuppernongs
squash blossoms   nightingales
they spread open hands
on the globes of their bellies

where fluttering life treads water

Ann Howells edited *Illya's Honey* for eighteen years. She has been named a Distinguished Poet of Dallas. Recent books: *So Long As We Speak Their Names* (Kelsay Books, 2019) and *Painting the Pinwheel Sky* (Assure Press, 2020). Chapbooks *Black Crow in Flight* and *Softly Beating Wings* were published through contests.

Terrarium

by Valeka Cruz

Plants hang from the ceiling
white veined tendrils brush my arm
and   the back of my neck while
I sit on the tufted green velvet sofa
rusty screens on unwashed windows
cast   an amber glow on the room.
it is enchanting
it is   ethereal
the plants   breathe
the plants   move

in the corner of the room   surrounded
by curled sepia photos pinned to the wall
is a large glass domed terrarium filled
with ferns and moss pebbles and dirt
water droplets cling inside and
slowly   trickle onto fuzzy
tightlywrappedtendrils

I close my eyes as vines wrap
around my ankles and arms
moss envelope me in sultry
green softness my feet burrow
into the dirt pebbles cool
against my toes
droplets fall   on my bare skin and eyelashes

I fall asleep in the warm   suddenness
the plants feel me   breathe
the plants hear me move
I am enchanting
I glow   in the amber   light
I am   ethereal

Valeka Cruz is a writer, essayist, and poet living in Austin, Texas. Her
work has been published in various online publications and journals
including the Boundless 2021 Anthology.

Buddha Grows within Her

by Jyotirmoy Sil

Struck in Chrome browsings,
Senility looms in the spleen.
Some walls of a humid alley
Covered with cheap advertisements,
Carefully woven like spider webs.
Thorns of slurs
Or soaked handkerchiefs,
Poised against her humid eyes.

When someone pierced through her skin
And drew a window in her pinjar,
And left
With the silent footsteps of a cat.
Moments eroded her
She flew into a river.

Since then...
Suffocated slurs,
Sounds of murmurs,
A few alphabets
Systolic chords;
Some broken hemispheres.

With every cruelly distorted rhyme
An insidious Buddha grows within her,
To mend the circle
Of her chaotic refrain.

Jyotirmoy Sil is a dilettante poet. Presently he is an Assistant Professor of English in Malda College, West Bengal. His poems have been published in *Muse India* , *Madras Courier* , *Spillwords*, and *International Times*.

Lonelier than the First Day of School
by Stephen Douglas Wright

Remember how big the bus was?
Growling, yellow elephant
Red light tusks
Piercing the morning cold

You could see your breath
Appear and disappear
As the elephant ambled forward
Beckon you enter its mouth
Unleashed its terraced tongue;
First step up too high for little legs

How did you feel
Crawling into the belly
Of the snarling beast
Looking back at mom
The elephant, leviathan, digested you,
Slurped away your face's color
Stomach acid churning it
Into its own yellow skin
As it swam down the street?
Can you recall?
Were the kids mean or nice?
Did you cry, or did you and the others
Watch another
Scour the room for mother,
Piss himself and whimper?
How did you survive?
You had not felt so small
In a world so big
Since expulsion from the womb
Did you dig up a shield or breastplate?
From beneath the wood chips

Stowed away by the wiser, older kids,
Between the slide and swing set?

After recess' recession
And the passing of lunch,
You scribbled in art class
Triangles, squares, circles,
And such

Did your crayon wax coalesce?
Into the beginnings of a poem
Transfiguring blue shapes
Into longings for home?
You drew a long line in red,
Four other lines perpendicular,
On the etchings of a knee
A tear dropping off a face

At recess
You had scraped your legs,
Pushed aside by boys
In a mad dash to be first
In the line
Back into the classroom;
Was that your first-time bleeding?

Face chalk white
Knees raspberry rouge
Lonelier than the first day of school

Stephen Douglas Wright is a poet, playwright and author from the United States, currently living in Taiwan. His work has appeared in the USA and abroad, and was previously published in Boundless 2021. You can learn more about his work at stephendouglaswright.com

unnamed

by Zairja

they got the dragon, Loong, from the flag of the Qing dynasty
tattooed back home in Manila,
said it was a gang thing but that may have been a bluff,
and I wanted badly to trace the scales along the fur of their forearm,
while the charming rasp of a voice that's been smoking since it was 10
told me this place of mesquite and mosquitoes was as boring
as our job counting heads in the colonias.
so we went about our census duties,
looking like a couple of Mormon missionaries,
lean frames in oversized attire,
stained cuffs from Milano's marinara.
at the last trailer-home, I recited the Spanish on the questionnaire,
then asked the lady in the doorway about her esposa. ¿esposa?
she cocked her head and laughed -- ah, esposo.
only a vowel to me, ignorant as I am.
later, as we lay, seats back, in my old Toyota,
I've already forgot the distinction, meaning only to kiss
their small, plain face carried with such ease,
that I could carry it as gently as our lips now touching,
no boxes to check or hovering questions –
only the certainty of skin to skin.
we stop as soon as we begin
because I was stupid and afraid.
you never come for coffee at savory perks or wait for me at the skating rink after work.
another decade, I'm taking census of the dirt.
new identities and orientations, my sister's partner's pronouns,
new checkboxes and new sounds,
and I remember these all the same,
but all I want is to remember their name.

Zairja writes poems, songs, stories, and instructions for computers. Zairja is inspired by the many permutations along the Rio Grande, from Brownsville to Albuquerque. Zairja wants to connect with poets and will not collect any personal information.

Go Ahead Throw It At My Brown Face Gender Fluid Macho Masculine Glitter Infested DSL Smile

by Luis Lopez-Maldonado

I mean, porque no right? since danza and poesia remind myself of my worth remind myself what I am capable of what I am who I am what I have done will do, is not only fucking wonderfully fabulous but it's very humbling you know, to help close the pipeline from classroom to juvie from virgin to slut from love to hate, you know math? you know numbers? well here are some good ones for you: in India there are 106 rapes per day, in general like in our communities on like this earth 2 children are sold every minute, in good ole patriotic America someone dies every 12 seconds, but hey who's counting. so yeah, go ahead and throw your homophobic racist uneducated spit on my carita hermosa de miel y mecos que brilla como sol mata como cancer, because ain't nobody's spit ever hurt anybody y porque tambien tengo que caminar with chin up hands in fists toenails the color of blood, not because I have to represent and survive and inspire but because I fucking feel like it and I almost forgot to close with a metaphor: because metaphor equals real poetry so here you go: I am a bike a bus a train, my wolf snout my snake skin my lion roar, I float I fly I disappear into blackness into racism into homophobia into the crack between overeducated and genius.

Luis Lopez-Maldonado is a Xicanx poeta, playwright, dancer, choreographer, and educator. His work has been seen in *The American Poetry Review*, *Foglifter*, *The Packinghouse Review*, *Public Pool*, and *Latina Outsiders: Remaking Latina Identity*, among many others. He earned a Master of Arts degree in Dance from Florida State University, and a Master of Fine Arts degree in Creative Writing from the University of Notre Dame. He is currently adding his glitter to the Land of Enchantment, working for the public education system as a Bilingual and Special Education Teacher.

Astronomical

by Jonathan Fletcher

Anytime I watch a private rocket launch on my laptop,
smoke mushroom from the cosmodrome, the spacecraft
enter the stratosphere, the passengers float about the ship,

I am reminded that in our universe, which is

13.8 billion years old,
93 trillion light years wide,
2 million degrees Kelvin,

there are more than

200 billion trillion stars,
700 quintillion planets,
2 trillion galaxies,

yet only 2,755 billionaires on a planet of 7.9 billion people,

most of whom will never get a chance to experience space,
many for whom the cost of food, shelter, and healthcare,
like the price of a single ticket aboard, is sky-high,

astronomical.

Although originally from San Antonio, Texas, **Jonathan Fletcher**
currently resides in New York City, where he is pursuing a Master of Fine
Arts in Creative Writing in Poetry at Columbia University's School of the
Arts. He has been published in *Arts Alive San Antonio*, *FlowerSong Press*,
Lone Stars; University of Texas Rio Grande Valley's literary magazine,
riverSedge; Our Lady of the Lake University's literary journal, *The Thing
Itself*, *TEJASCOVIDO; and Voice de la Luna.*

They ask us to write to raise awareness
by Rebecca Granado

I.

Awareness to whom
To the ones who happen to stumble
upon the words

The words on paper
you don't like the sound of it
the sound of the words out loud
only mean something when
someone more important gives them meaning

Your fetish of latinas with
long hair and big asses
and snatched waists
who cook good and speak
a language of colonizers

It turns you on
my stylish eyebrows
detract from the experiences in my heart
I'm just a chola to you,
but im a dumb Mexican to them
and a chicana to smart for her
own good to those over there

You label me because
that is what society loves
slap me with your words
but not on paper

The words that penetrate your heart
the ones that leave your mouth
the mouth you
don't put meat into

Because meat, it's not love
but desert wildlife shows you love
by giving you sustenance
as you journey through what
feels like an endless labyrinth to get home

II.

It was 5am when I heard the screeching of a lechuza, looked out my bedroom
window and saw it perched on the deck. I immediately woke up and got out of
bed and took a shower; praying in the shower for strength for the message the
lechuza was sending. I was due any day now and the new house was coming
along beautifully. Pero I knew that something wasn't right because of the owl.

The Canadian Customs had him. I finally got his call later that day. I couldn't
have this baby alone. The mortgage is due and the car needs gas. Pero the culeros
were flying him to Tamaulipas instead of Tijuana, his place of origin. Man they
can't even follow their own rules. Now what do I do? Pay 3 grand for him to get
back? I can't do that. It's all our savings so far.

The words had meaning all along, before my wounds would create this feeling
in you from afar for your poetic enjoyment and artsy critique I become a person
to you with that feeling that person is exploited for the story on paper to raise
awareness and here we are

III.

We need to move forward and forgive and forget
no one made you come here without permission
that's why minorities stay in their miserable situations que no
for not obeying the rules
an induced yawn because you heard it all before from these illegals
and the rolling of your eyes because I sound stupid to you

You love our beaches and our women
our food and the culture
we speak proper English and went
to high school and prom like you
we never broke the law
but I thought wetbacks didn't know anything
about wanting to be smart and have

careers to retire and watch their family grow
the kids playing in the backyard
during family gatherings
no we don't want that

Mojados walking thru dry government land
walls and cameras
invisible lines in the mesquites
triggering signals and booby traps to catch him
as he walked by
how dare we call this country home
the one they claim to be so precious
yet in its scarcity lie the evil of death lurking
thru thirst and hunger
if the snakes, scorpions, or spiders don't get you
before the migra gets their hands on you
Hollywood couldn't conjure up this script

Walking for days to save money on coyotes
avoiding 15 years in federal prison
Trying not to go into labor early from stress
Buying phone cards and money gram
7 days it took him
to Canada to the tip of México back
up to the good ole USA

Well I didn't believe him when he said he would
be back in time to see the baby born
Where there's a will there's a way
He cut her umbilical cord and held her
as they took their first and last daddy/daughter photo
The feds took him anyway
I became suicidal
I wanted to die as I looked at my beautiful baby
She smiled at me with her dad's eyes
I had to live
I had to keep going

As we live off acronyms
TANF, HUD, SNAP, WIC, SSI
It's not them draining the system

It's the citizens of this country
My own country had backstabbed me
My own land had betrayed me

The deep pain
Of watching your child
Grow up without a father
Because of laws
Meant to protect
The years we can't get back
The missed joy of her dad watching
her grow into the beautiful 17 year old she has become
The mending of hearts it will take
to get these two on track as father and daughter
The part of the story no one hears or feels until
it's put on paper and someone with authority gives it meaning

Rebecca Granado is an underground writer and published author with a Master of Science in Marriage and Family Therapy (MFT) and Addictions Studies. She is an Ordained Minister, Notary Public and a Relationship and Sex Coach. Her writings reflect her personal life journey; as she wishes to share these rough, rugged, and Raw memories.

THOUGH WE TRY

by Nathan Brown

~ for Larry Martin

When walls are built
for the proprietary
purposes of people
who believe we can
own pieces of land,

Nature begins its act
of reclamation the very
moment one's completed,

careful to move slowly enough
that the fool who built the thing
will not perceive the inevitable.

Nathan Brown is an author, songwriter, and award-winning poet living in Wimberley, Texas. He holds a PhD in English and Journalism from the University of Oklahoma. He served as Poet Laureate for Oklahoma in 2013/14 and now travels full time performing readings, concerts, workshops and speaking on creativity, poetry, and songwriting.

HALVES
by Dee Allen

America's
Own Africans exist
In halves: One, surviving in
Slums. Other, facing
Bars.

W:10.14.21

Dee Allen is an African-Italian performance poet based in Oakland, California. Author of 7 books--*Boneyard, Unwritten Law, Stormwater, Skeletal Black, Elohi Unitsi* and coming in February 2022, *Rusty Gallows: Passages Against Hate and Plans*--and 43 anthology appearances under his figurative belt so far.

Save the Marmots!

by Terry Allen

This is all I have. I'm sorry. I'd gladly give more if I had it.

We all do what we can.

It seems like a worthy cause...

Oh, it is.

Support the Save the Marmot Wildlife Fund.!

Oh, yes.

I don't know much about it, really. It's hard to keep up on everything.

It is.

Although I do my best. I read a bit here and there, and I watch news programming now and then just to find out what's going on in the world. Marmots are foxlike animals, aren't they? Sort of like a short, wild dog sort of thing?

Let me help you. A marmot is a rather large ground squirrel, actually. There are fifteen species found in Asia, Europe and North America, if I'm not mistaken

No, you're quite right. I remember now. You've got your Alaska Marmot and your Alpine Marmot and your Black Capped Marmot from eastern Siberia.

With each donation of $20, we give you a t-shirt with a picture of a marmot, riding a bicycle.

Are they circus animals?

Not in the least. Just try getting a Himalayan Marmot to do acrobatics and sleight of hand and see what happens.

Perhaps the Vancouver Island Marmot would be capable.

Well yes. The Vancouver Island Marmot is another matter entirely. But not the Himalayan Marmot?

Oh, heaven's no.

Do you take checks?

Oh, yes, with proper identification, of course, and a $15 check service fee.

Terry Allen was born in Australia and grew up in Kansas City, Missouri. He is an emeritus professor of Theatre Arts at the University of Wisconsin-Eau Claire, where he taught acting, directing and playwriting. He is the author of *Monsters in the Rain* and *Art Work*.

Erev Rosh Hashanah Masked Distanced Outdoor Dinner*
by Gerard Sarnat MD

Fraught beyond usual combo
Of cheer anticipating New Year
Family and friends feasting together

Plus tiny bit of underlying strife regards
Who's responsible for what better-than-your
Dishes, which children are causing that ruckus

Now many adults wanna speed patriarch's service
Along because they simply do not buy kosheryness
—Never heard of using okra or squash for our rituals—

Pomegranates are really the only legitimate way to go for
All of us Eastern European Old Country-derived Ashkenazis
Don't give nada hoot about more recent Holy Land generations

Well as their desert rituals though they sure know how to blow shofars.

*Please take above fun with grain of sugar, used last night instead of routine Shabbat
salt to dab once-a-year hunks round challah which replaces standard fare.

Gerard Sarnat MD's authored *HOMELESS CHRONICLES*, *Disputes*, *17s*, *Melting Ice King*. Gerry's published by Gargoyle, Newark Public Library, Blue Minaret, North Meridian Review, Columbia, Penn, Harvard, Brown, Stanford, Main Street Rag, New Delta Review, Northampton Review, New Haven Institute, Buddhist Review, American Journal Poetry, Poetry Quarterly, Brooklyn Review, LA Review, SF Magazine, NY Times.

Poet

by Anthony Ripp

In the case of my madness, it's been determined, it's a simple explanation,
I'm a poet.
Who dries his clothes out in the sun
to the tune of "Singing in the rain."

Naked, in the meantime,
I eat television dinners,
play the radio loudly,
and wonder at the bookmark in my pocket calendar.
What day is it?
I haven't missed the show have I?
On Jackson and 1st,
with what's her name?

Anthony Ripp considers himself a storyteller who writes his best material on the open road or sitting in the middle of an ocean in a remote part of the world. He takes his inspiration from real life events and enjoys featuring the beauty that is attached to the rusty side of life. Anthony states that he does not write to make a point, he writes to make the listeners feel something.

Punk Lover

by Bidisha Chakraborty

Possess a scholarly shell,
Professor of Philosophy, rests as your designation
You chant Hegelian hymns and ethical symbiosis
Neither strict to logic, nor rationalism
You bear a high academic persona
Who knows you are a hardcore punk?
Who knows you adore tattoos in your arms?
Your tattoos are lucky but not am I
A devout follower of punk melodies
You decor your playlists with jazz and rock
Your playlists have space but not have I
You quickly conquered the ethical thoughts,
Of British and French philosophies,
Discarding my ethics of love,
Blaming them as futile melodies
Hey, my punk lover
What are these, the translucent curtains of egoism?
These are venomous, arousing cyclones of ignorance
Hey, my punk lover, remove this Berlin wall
This opaque is an aesthetic cataract
I have gulped you within me,
If you strip off my flesh,
You will discover another you,
Hey, my punk lover devour me to amnesia
Your tattoos are lucky, but not am I
To my Philosopher,
My punk lover

Bidisha Chakraborty is a post graduate student in English Language and Literature from University of Calcutta. She is currently pursuing her B.Ed degree, a pedagogic research course from Adamas University, Calcutta. Her area of interests prevails in creative writing and she is a poet by passion. Bidisha aspires to establish herself as a brilliant writer in her future endeavors.

EVALUATION OF A K.A.A.T MEOW

by Abdulrazaq Salihu

Meow
(In this recapitulation; we all know our fur by heart)
And melts our paws into SightTwoMiceChaseTwoMice gaff
With a body of brass liquid failing
Before you fast forward the earth to where you have no pets,
Wear a metallic bi-stripes of iron and ore
Take your body into a leaf a soil and you're close to time traveling
The body is a man, your body is only another
Genus of Homo fitting so perfectly into a panthera
And I'm the first to carry a new name into an evolution
Of countless evaluations—you're me in so many ways;
Burnt clay; fidgeting an ozone of cosmo hereditary—
You're me in so many ways; meow and mirrors are only
Collected pieces of shattered identities.

Abdulrazaq Salihu is a Nigerian 17 year old poet ,Spoken word artist and writer. He was the winner of most valuable contestant (male) at HIASFEST 2021, First runner up for spoken poetry and second runner up for on the spot poetry contest. He is a member of the hilltop creative arts foundation and also an organizer of HIASFEST The biggest teen literary event in Africa). He has some of his poems published/upcoming in SHAGAZ anthology; an Indian Anthology that won fastest compiled anthology, Konya Shamsrumi magazine, Christmas tide, Waah re kisan, stories from the heart, Amulet poetry magazine, PineCone review, world voices magazine, Icefloe magazine and more. He believes that poetry is life!

Indoctrination

The fear of God is the beginning of wisdom
Proverbs 9:10 by Kelly Ann Ellis

Creep past these walls where roses climb
to watch over white-fenced fields outside.

Find a darksome room at the end of the hall
windows black with cadaverous flies
panes sealed shut and gray with grime.

This is the valley of dry bones:
Gehenna, Hades, the Lake of Fire.
This is where the bad folks go.

Forests grow locusts, rivers run blood.
charred by a basement furnace blast,
Structures fall like Lincoln logs

cut once from these evergreen
groves of pine that thrive, leave, breathe
in the sun beyond this dust-choked dusk.

Throw your shoulders into walls.
Rake roses raw with fingernails.
You will adapt to smoke at last

Picture a crumbled, coal-cured husk
emptied of after   bereft of before
Someone forgot and closed the door.

Someone forgot and closed the door.
Emptied of after   bereft of before
Picture a crumbled coal-cured husk

You will adapt to smoke at last,
roses raked raw from fingernails,
tracks of shoulders smudging walls.

In sun beyond this dust-choked dusk
groves of pine still thrive, leave, breathe.
Cut once from these evergreens,

structures fall like Lincoln logs
charred by a basement furnace blast.
Forests grow locusts, rivers run blood.

This is where the bad folks go:
Gehenna, Hades, the Lake of Fire—
This, the Valley of Dry Bones.
Panes sealed shut and gray with grime,
windows black with cadaverous flies,
Crouch in the dark-roomed end of the hall,

to watch the white-fenced fields outside
creep past these walls where roses climb.

Kelly Ann Ellis lives, writes, and works in Houston, Texas, where she is co-founder of hotpoet, Inc., a literary nonprofit dedicated to building community and supporting the work of artists and writers. She enjoys writing in all genres as a way to explore the world and her place in it.

⌘ My First Snowman was a Snow-woman and I Think I Loved Her

by Kai Coggin

It's spring now,
outside the dogwoods are bursting forth
their tiny crucifixions into a new season,
and I sit here in my cold office writing ritual
holding onto her memory in the chilly bite of daybreak,
remembering the shape of her,
remembering her rotund beauty,
the perfection of her roundness breaking every social norm,
the rounder the better, yes, bigger still,
I sing her circumference here,
wide snow-woman,
I made her giant,
the snow-packed balls of her impermanence
stacked up with my child-like wonder.

She was my first,
my only snowman ever made
so of course, I made her a woman,
of course, I made her in the likeness of all I love,
and it took 41 years to reach a moment like this,
the circumstance of legitimate snow never reaching Bangkok or Houston,
but this freak Arkansas blizzard shaped opportunity out of the air,
feet of snow staying for a week of snow
brought me to roll her into being,
heavy and life-like,
frozen but her face full of warmth,
I think of her smile now and my heart melts.

Let me take it back a few weeks,
back to that moment fresh fallen and white,
inches of packy snow begging to be made memorable,
and honestly I had no idea
how a snowman really worked,
how the snowflake logistics actually transpired into a life.

Snow really rolls.
Yes, just like in the movies— it rolls,
and I started at the top of our modest driveway hill,
rolling a handful down the slope and the molecular magic
that folded ice crystals into a sphere just suddenly
shaped into the bottom of her, foundational,
sturdy like woman are, wide and prepared
for all that was to be set on her frame,
and she was waiting, forming,
yet to be named.
Three feet across, or maybe more,
was the size of her beginning,
the mountain of her that I would build upon,
now standing on solid ground perched to become,
and I trudged snowy wet footsteps up the hill
to manifest her middle from the path before me,
another handful rolled down,
and rolled down and rolled,
gravity creating
a bigger and bigger ball of her,
wet and heavy at the perfect freeze,
it took everything for me to lift this piece of her
but I did it, I knew she was there, I could feel her,
and with the strength summoned suddenly there was her body,
two perfectly stacked snowballs,
infinity standing from molecules of water,
a small avalanche shaped with my hands, waiting for a head.

Her head came from halfway up the hill, rolled and rolled,
set atop the stack and there she was,
the complete creation,
a wonder in white,
my gloveless hands smoothed her edges,
shaped her three-stack form into one solid woman,
her globes merging into one, and my world forever changed.

I ran inside to get her clothes,
a flowered top-hat and my favorite bright scarf from Paris,
I grabbed two long-stemmed roses from the Valentine's vase,
and knew they would be perfect for her arms,
rose-petal hands,

for her face I raided the refrigerator,
found a handful of radishes and a carrot,
wanted her perishable and gorgeous,
bursting with warmth and color,
as my heart was bursting with this new joy.

Within minutes she was finished,
my darling snowy masterpiece,
radish eyes that shined like love itself,
carrot nose because that seems to be a standard snow rule,
her smile shaped from the curve of a twig,
radish buttons, and roses for arms,
the top-hat set on her snowy head and scarf wrapped around her
cold shoulders, and I swear she came alive.

I swear, she came alive,
and she was the most beautiful
snow-woman ever rolled into existence,
we called her Rosie and I even made up a little song
that is almost too embarrassing to even put into a poem,
but unabashed wonder does that to a person,
unlocks giddiness and pure joy,
I was a child at 41
dancing with my snow-woman,
and her rose-petal hands touched my cheeks
and I looked into her radish eyes,
and kissed her frosty face,
wanting this moment never to melt away.

And it's spring now,
and my beloved snow-woman
is a stream somewhere rushing in the wild,
but I can still see her in my mind's eye smiling,
her rose petals hands waving in the breeze,
the memory of her
frozen in my heart forever.

Kai Coggin (she/her) is the author of four poetry collections, most recently
Mining for Stardust (FlowerSong Press 2021) and INCANDESCENT
(Sibling Rivalry Press 2019). She is a queer woman of color who thinks

Black Lives Matter, a teaching artist in poetry with the Arkansas Arts Council and Arkansas Learning Through the Arts, and host of the longest running consecutive weekly open mic series in the country—Wednesday Night Poetry. Recently awarded the 2021 Governor's Arts Award and named "Best Poet in Arkansas" by the Arkansas Times, her fierce and powerful poetry has been nominated four times for The Pushcart Prize, as well as Bettering American Poetry 2015, and Best of the Net 2016, 2018, 2021—and chosen in 2022. Her poems have appeared or are forthcoming in POETRY, Cultural Weekly, SOLSTICE, Bellevue Literary Review, TAB, Entropy, SWWIM, Split This Rock, Sinister Wisdom, Lavender Review, Tupelo Press, West Trestle Review, and elsewhere. Coggin is Associate Editor at The Rise Up Review. She lives with her wife and their two adorable dogs in the valley of a small mountain in Hot Springs National Park, Arkansas

Sexist trope love doll fantasy

by Mike Zone

Androgynous albino
a plethora of neon-colored wigs
zippered eyes
choosing what to see
whether imaginary or daybreak surgical deceit
operation blues
orifices aplenty doesn't matter where
just when
okay, not the hands… too bizarre
buckles for infliction
bound in straps
duct tape saggy chest with cigarette in the center
mouth smelling like cheap vodka and chemotherapy
said "thought you were a muse…"
"No, I'm amused"
something unreal giggled

Mike Zone is the Editor in Chief of Dumpster Fire Press, the author of *Shedding Dark Places (almost), One Hell of a Muse, A Farewell to Big Ideas* and *Void Beneath the Skin*, as well as coauthor of *The Grind.* frequent contributor to Alien Buddha Press and Mad Swirl. His work has been featured in: Horror Sleaze Trash, Better Than Starbucks, Piker Press, Punk Noir Magazine, Synchronized Chaos, Outlaw Poetry and Cult Culture magazine.

A Self-Starter's Guide to Economic Independence
by Abigail Carl-Klassen

Start-up is just another word for family

money. It doesn't matter what the question is

the answer is always,

"It was just

a small

loan

a small

asset

a small

injection of capital

a small

deficit

a little

gift

a little

help

a little

networking

a little

leverage

an early

Inheritance."

Abigail Carl-Klassen grew up in the oilfields of the Permian Basin and is a writer, poet, educator, translator, and activist living in El Paso Texas.

Laundry Day

by John C. Mannone

My cell phone clock fails to alarm.
I don't have a Clue why. Sorry. It's a game
my old phone has been playing.
Some things just stop working.

I lather Gillette gel and shave,
wash with body soap, then dry
and dress before shuffling down
the hallway to the kitchen for coffee.

It's only nine but too late for the stale
pastry and the 5 a.m. coffee, now tepid,
and weak as usual. I keep my mouth shut;
don't want to tangle with the cook

lest she'd nail my hide to the wall
like a raccoon skin rug. But I slip
out, and drive to the nearest Starbucks
before zooming back in a frizz. My hair,

what little is left of it, is disheveled
like ragweed but I wear my mother's
        smile… and finish my laundry
        at the homeless shelter.

John C. Mannone has poems in *Windhover, North Dakota Quarterly, Poetry South, Azahares Spanish Language Literary Magazine, Somos en escrito,* and others. He was awarded a Jean Ritchie Fellowship (2017) in Appalachian literature. He's the poetry editor for *Abyss & Apex.* A retired physics professor, John lives in Knoxville, Tennessee.

Disco

by Gerald Cedillo

American DJs staged a great coup against democracy
when they barred their airwaves and allowed disco to die.

I know because at Chapultepec the dishwashers shout
over a steam-hiss water hose all the Bee Gees biggest hits.

It's water pruned hands and tired knees, not popped collar
dreams and polyester leisure suits, but the music makes all

things possible. 1970's rhythm with spanish accent falsetto,
night fever! night fever!— proves the rest of the world

wasn't wrong in keeping this message alive. Not glitter,
spandex, not neon-lit floors, just unhesitating love.

Weekends, my aunts wove a bright orange extension cord
through grandma's kitchen and at the end was a boombox

sitting on the dirt driveway with a stack of cassette tapes.
Selena's final concert opens this way, I remember. My first

quinceanera, after the teens and young couples tired out
and left the rented hall, the parents simply continued past

midnight, shuffling to Rod Stewart and the Commodores.
In Mexico City, the all night discoteca advertised as 24/8.

Are there silent backhouses of restaurants in this nation?
Our busboy swings his hips around tables as he picks up.

The cook's metal tongs hit her caldero like heel clicks
on a raised stage. A wire brush spins inside a metal pot,

chk-chk-chk, like starched fabric pressed against a body,
inching up like a dress across an intent leg against a body.

Kitchens claim the heart of the home, home a cornerstone
of a peoples— blues people, ballad people, gente llorando—

no wonder days multiply into infernos, flagrant emotions
ring bells in our chest. We weep openly, we celebrate,

and we beg for a little more heaven, here, not in whispers
anymore, no speakeasy affairs, but in full-throated song.

Gerald Cedillo is from Houston, Texas where he attended the University of St. Thomas and studied Creative Writing at the University of Houston. He has taught theater, performance poetry, and writing. He has been a literary event organizer, was on the board of Houston's legendary week-long poetry festival, The Word Around Town, and is a part of many erstwhile writing groups such as The Balcony Poets and The Shout. He currently works for the publishing venture The Atomic Underground.

Salmon Sunrise

by PW Covington

She is flying off
Into salmon glowing cloudy sunrise
Low ceiling cielo
From the airbase
At the base
Of ancient mountain

And my coffee, brewed at home
Will not be cooled
By the time she lands in Houston
Fossils, constellations, poetry
Time travel never fails to leave its mark
Remember pines and honeysuckle evenings
When seasons served as bookends
Semesters
Catalogs
Containers of our ossuary days together

Disconnected internet and power lines
Sonatas in the key of entropy play
Above the choking ceiling morning burning
Pink and orange window shade left open
She slips sunglasses on
And orders wine

PW Covington's collection "North Beach and Other Stories" was named a Finalist in LGBTQ+ Fiction by the International Book Awards in 2019. Covington lives in Northern New Mexico, just off Historic Route 66.

www.PWCovington.com

Lingering at Hainan

by Hei Feng, translated by Wang Ping

Today I just want a bowl of noodles
The coconut breeze is as soft as the southern music
    A piece of glass, so blue

Peace between water and salt

    Pieces of paper are flying
    White birds whirling, more real than paper

    In a space no one can reach

Deep sleep...
    But today I
Just want a bowl of noodles

I enter the island through my last grains of rice from Hubei
I can't deny: I see the island's sky
    "Swishing—" into the landscape of post-industrial country

But today
When the black screen is shut off from the "future"
    Today all day
I gaze at the coconut. My attention goes
To the smooth coconut
    --sour, perhaps
But I don't care

For a whole day today, I feel clean

At dusk I borrow a bird's nest for the night
I dream of birds flying around my dreams
Kakakakaka
    The birds didn't return to their nest
I dream my dreams are hatching their eggs

A bird
   Flying
In sixth dimensional space
Tonight
   I can't close my eyes
Tonight
I think about the bird
More than my wife
Tonight I go over my "lessons" word by word
Tonight, I'm hungry, but I refuse to eat the eggs

The sun shines on me lightly
Like a beach in mirage, after the tide

I learn to wade into the hard water of the self
I wake up

The moon is high
The sun is shallow

逗留海南

这一天，我只想吃一碗面
虽然椰风与南韵柔软
   一块玻璃很蓝

水与盐平静

  虽然有一些纸在飞
  一些比纸更真的白鸟在摇

  在触及不到的一片空间里

深睡眠……
   然而，这一天我
只想吃一碗面

我用最后的几粒湖北大米进入岛屿
不能否认，我看见了岛屿的天空
"眚——"的推进的国家后工业社会的前景

81

而这一天
在关闭"前景"的黑屏的这一天
　　　　整整一天
我只端详椰子。我只关心近处的
一颗光滑椰子
　　　　　——它也许很酸
但我不怕这种"酸"

而这一整天，我干净
傍晚我在岛语之外借鸟窝过夜
我梦见鸟嘎嘎嘎嘎嘎嘎嘎嘎叫着裛绕着我的
梦境飞

　　　　鸟终夜不归
我的梦孵化鸟蛋

一只鸟
在第6维
　　　　飞

这一夜
　　　我彻夜无眠

这一夜我思念一只鸟
胜过妻子
这一夜我反复温习"功课"
这一夜，饥饿。但我不吃鸟蛋

太阳很浅地照我
犹如蜃气中的退潮的沙滩

我学习并涉过自己坚硬的水
我醒了

月亮很高
太阳很浅
　　　　　　1994.12作 2020.11.7修订

82

That Day

by Hei Feng, translated by Wang Ping

So much anxiety after Mother was buried
So much fear
Under the white sun

You died, Mother
My wound was buried with your body
Your black bones have my batting sticks

That day
I carried the wind
I carried white eyes

Empty basket

That day, I was empty
That day, I was weightless
That day, I was all bones
That day, I was full of fear

My sister was still young
My other sister was married
I went out to gather vegetables for pigs

Lilies, shepard purse, spinach
Come out, hurry
Alfafa, plantain, ground covers
Don't hide yourselves
I'm coming

Seek
Seek seek seek seek
I filled half of my basket

The sun entered the earth
My little sister wanted her mother

Don't be afraid
Big brother will take you home

Brother, your hand is cold
Brother, you're crying
Sister, you have no idea
what kind of fear I have in my heart
That day
The world changed
The white sun pushed me down
Water carried me
----away

That day, I was all bones
That day, I was weightless
That day, I was empty
That day, I was afraid
The world was a net full of holes

那天……

葬了母亲好惊慌
葬了母亲怕
白太阳

母亲你死去
体内有我的伤
你的黑骨里
有我的木棒

那天
我提着风
我提着白眼

空竹篮

那天，我空
那天，我轻
那天，我瘦

那天，我多么慌

妹妹小
姊姊出嫁了
我去找猪草

黄花菜地米菜耳朵菜
你们快出来
苜蓿草车前草被褥草
你们不要
我来找

找
找找找找找……
找了半篮草

太阳落土
妹妹找母

不怕
哥哥带你回家

哥哥你手好凉
哥哥你哭了
妹妹你哪知道
哥哥心里好慌

那天
目光异样
白太阳将我推倒
水载我
——流走

那天，我瘦
那天，我轻
那天，我空
那天，我多么慌
世界是一个透风的网

2006. 2. 13作 2017. 3. 16修订

By the Window

Huang Lihai, translated by Wang Ping

It just snowed
As if all the love in this world had fallen on earth

You sit by the window
Crashing into light
How crispy is the sun
As if you had just received the most delightful gift

Light travels through your thoughts
Thinner, quieter
Like a child, not knowing he's so loved

窗下

这里刚下过一场雪
仿佛人间的爱都落到低处

你坐在窗下
窗子被阳光突然撞响
多/么干脆的阳光呀
仿佛你一生不可多得的喜悦

光线在你的思想中
越来越稀薄 越来越
安静 你像一个孩子
一无所知地被人深深爱着

Huang Lihai: poet from the most southern part of China, editor in chief for *China and West Poetry* Journal, and the chair for "Poetry and People International Lifetime Achievement Award." He has published hundreds of great poets around the world since 2005, and awarded great poets like ngénio de Andrade (Portugal), Derek Walcott (St. Lucia), Peng Yanjiao (China), Zhang Shuguang (China), Lan Lan (China), Anna Lysyanska (Russia), Tomas Tranströmer (Sweden), Tomaz Salamund (Slovenia), Dong Dangzi (China), Adam Zagajewski (Poland), Xi Chuan (China), Rita Dove (USA), and George Szirtes. This year's award is going to Gary Snyder (USA).

His name Lihai 礼孩 means gift child. This poet is a gift for the world.

Notes from Alxa Right Banner

Wen Gu, translated by Wang Ping

1.   Mandela Mountain Range

Rain breaks on black rocks
Stars fall, one by one, on blue stones

A thousand years, ten thousand years, and the wind sings:
"Ten Thousand, one thousand, each night, same difference."

History storms out of the camels' backs
Cooking fragrance lingers between goats' lips

Don't ask the secrets of my ancestors
Their thunder is carved on the faces of these rocks

2.   Walking to Mount Mandela

The eagle carries blue sky and drops it on the ridge of the Mandela

White clouds ride on the heads of mountain goats
An elk runs into the rock, dressed in flowers
Moonlight trickles out of stones

Wind flows like a stream
Telling a story

Of the ancient nomads
My ancestors lived here
Where tall grasses grow

3.   The Wolves Broke the Gazelle's neck

Time spasms and bends
Starlight cuts the veins of basalt

Dusk is drowned in blood

A thousand peaks kneel down
Camels spit out half-chewed grass
Tears hang on thorny vines

To mourn the fallen gazelle

When Mount Mandela turned purple
A wolf bit into a gazelle's throat

A story of life and death, carved on the rock
Too heavy to bear, for the land of Alxa

4. **Sunset on Mount Yabulai**

On the desk of Mount Yabulai
Stars burnt into piles of ashes

Ten thousand years, the sky
Has inhaled the time

If I fall asleep tonight
You'll see a cistanche root tomorrow
Dark, deep in the earth

5. **Rock Painting, Horse Riders and Eagle**

Trust the eagle Leading my ancestors
Out of the rocks' sky

Trust the hunter's arrow
Penetrating the night silence

Trust the grasses under the horse
Holding onto the bending river
Lambs and fouls on the bank of a stream
Step into a white cloud reflection

Trust the zigzagging time, waves like schools of fish bubbling

Trust the stream, broken by horse hooves
Splashing out of the rocks
Shining in the moonlight

The ancestors' faces, solemn and resolute
Weighing down the noise of grasses

6.   Crossing the Gobi

Stars gnaw at the sky
A book full of holes

The rock painting repairs it
Into a myth, with clouds

Eagles carry stars on their backs
Cattle carry wind and rain on their backs
Mount Mandela, you carry sentient beings, heavier than rocks, towards our destiny

This is the secret, leaked from the sky book
This is the footnotes in the dictionary of time
This is the gossip of gods

Thunder's carriage grinds the uneven road

Let's go! Euphorbia's fiery tails
Are seeking suoyang—desert roots
Slithering like black pythons under the Gobi

7.   Rock Painting, Village

When our sky congeals into a giant rock
The setting sun lights our village with a campfire
18 tents open 18 nights
The moon hangs like a breast

Sleep! Wild flowers blossom in the fields
Outside the tents, animals lie in the mist

No paradise is more beautiful than this place
Even gods are envious of these muscled men

Time blows by like a river
Sending a fallen leaf to a distant place
As we snore away in beds

8. The Handprints on the Tanlaogaole Rocks

On the ridge of Taolangaolei
A pair of hands are talking

Bleeding fingers
Tell a weeping story

A pair of hands scratched the rock face
Then reached into the sun
To brand her fire on the rock

A pair of hands reached into the moon
Washing away old sorrow and hate

Ten fingers dug into the flesh of the rock
Its blood tells the story of hunting, grazing, life, children, death and wars

Then he rolled up his sleeves
To grab meat, pull his bow, chase animals, sharpen his stone arrows

Till he fell asleep with the sheep and cattle, only the hands still awake on the rock

9. Rock Painting, Yaks

Night is still warm in the deep of rocks
The sun has left us, but the flesh is still burning

Enough heat to lift the giant boulder
But the rock holds the world steady
With its solid force

Now the whole mountain becomes the base of a bull
The mines rumble with stars
We've inherited the bone marrow of our ancestors
History will burst through the crack
When time comes

Let it cool down ! Let ambition cool against the rock wall
Every stone
Has gone through the burning

10.   Rock Painting, Hunter, Hunting Dogs, Gazelles

A gentle south wind pushes
Brown deer past the blue rocks

In cold winter, my starved ancestors follow
The deer with bows and arrows

They hunted, set up tents with tree branches
Washed their bloody hands in the river
Warming themselves over the fire at sunset

At dusk, they danced
With the campfire smoke
Then vanished into the rocks

Their labor continued
As symbols and images of the rock painting

When night wind blows
Their thin bodies
Tremble in the rocks
Rustling like dry leaves

Wen Gu, editor of *The Grassland Journal,* his 18 poetry books include *Wen Gu Selected Poems, Low Fire, Signature under Eagle Claws, Fire Under the Sunset, Bird Tribe* and others. Recipient of many poetry awards, and his poems have been translated into English, Mongolian, Japanese and others.

FROM OUR EDITORS

Constructions

by Gina Duran

My father constructed skyscrapers and bridges and the metro.
He is much larger than you know.
My father constructed the overpasses we drive under, everyday.
My father constructed freeways we drive over, everyday.

When I take the metro into LA, I don't just see grandiose cathedral tiled ceilings and long tunnels to destinations known and unknown, I see tunnels into memories that are known and unknown.

As a child we would pass through grand freeway bridges into San Diego or San Clemente or San Bernardino, and my father would stick his thick calloused hand towards them and announce *I built that.* It didn't matter how many times we passed it, he would say it every time. And every time we were supposed to pay attention and basque in the glory of his creation.

He fell so many times and avoided many cars. He reached the heavens on top of scaffoldings and planks of wood. He built a launch pad to send rockets to touch the stars.

Perhaps, he was great. And when I walk into the vastness of his greatness I feel my tiny hand wrapped around his thumb. I imagine him lifting me off my feet with his fingers as he counted my pull-ups. I imagine grasping the door panel with my fingertips—to chimney climb the hallway— like he taught me. I run my toes in the sand of the beach, knowing I can swim, because he taught me in our pool on Beach street. He tossed me in like a toy, but not as far as he threw me across the living room—before he fattened my lip and injured my spine.

You need to do a better job of vacuuming. Your mom is in a bad mood and I don't want her to see this.(I did vacuum, it just wasn't to his liking.)

Do it again. He slapped me in the face, knocking me to the floor. I crawled on my back to hide under the coffee table, but he grabbed me by the collar next to my throat, strangling my new sweater. I thought he was going to choke me. He slapped me again. I kicked and got him in the balls. Suddenly, his eyes grew robotic and his face did something still with fury. He lifted me and flung me like a small sack with limbs. I wasn't a human. I was a purple cotton knit sweater.

I slid across the floor just in front of the stairs. My fibers wrapped up with the carpet's, with a gentle sharp burn along my back. He lunged over my body and slapped my face repeatedly. I shrieked and went numb.

When he was done I was sad to see my brand new purple sweater was stretched around the neck and limp around the arms, already ruined that early Christmas morning. I just unwrapped it. I changed into my turquoise sweater, which brought out the blues in my bruised cheek, before going to Grandma's house. It was just a hop over the wall, past Grandpa's car parts, and his old office building. The chickens scattered about while the rooster crowed from the tree. I wanted to tell Grandma what happened, but she didn't say anything.

She grounded up the salt and herbs with molcajete then rolled out the tortillas like she did everyday. I sat on the stool at the counter and watched as she talked to me as if my wounds were invisible. I felt invisible.

She mashed beans and brought out beef from the last butchered cow, stored in the freezer. (It might have been MooGa, my favorite cow friend.) I watched her stir and season. She looked into my face and asked what I got for Christmas. It made me angry. I was tired of being invisible and not talking about being whipped and tossed like trash. I was tired of people ignoring me. I was tired of everyone taking their shit out on me. I was 10 and it was Christmas.

I don't know. What do you think? I got this sweater and a purpla sweater that I really loved but my dad stretched it out when he threw me and gave me these bruises and a fat lip. That's what I got for Christmas. But you look at me like nothing is there, like it's a dream or a nightmare. Like it's not even real. Do you even see me? Your son did this to me. Do you even see me? Don't act like it's a lie. It's real. It's on my face. Why are you acting like everything is normal? Your son did this. Are you proud of him?

She looked up at me and said *I see it. I know it's real. I just thought I should mind my own business, so I didn't say anything.* I waited for more but she went back to cooking, so I got off the stool and went home.

My mom saw me and looked at my face. *Oh, your dad told me you were upset because he spanked you.*

He hit me in the face over and over again.

He said he didn't hit you hard. Those are just busted capillaries from stress. Go to your room.

That's when I knew nobody was ever going to get me out of there. I went upstairs to my room and let the bed absorb me and my tears. I was always always going to be there. The walls grew closer and closer and the devil crept in with the shadows as he peered in through the cracks of my dreams—claiming them as nightmares. I prayed and prayed that God would save me. I promised I would be good, but the nightmares would take over until I woke in the cold of my pee soaked sheets, with my curtains torn off the window and over my head.

I was running in my nightmares again. Jumping off the rooftop in a desperate attempt to escape my father. My mom would spank me if I didn't wash everything, so I gathered everything in the middle of the night to wash up. Then I fell asleep on the hot pink carpeted floor.

The summer my youngest child left for college I told my father I didn't understand why my child hated their dad so much. I understood that he slapped her in the face and that I knew it was abusive, but the level of rage that existed in them was confusing. (But maybe my child was just ready to leave what I didn't know how to leave yet). I told him how I remembered him throwing me across the living room, but I didn't remember feeling that level of rage. He stopped me and lifted himself up from his chair with a deep scowling brow. *I never hit you. All I ever did was hold you and love you.*

That was the last conversation I ever had with him.

Gina Duran was born in Camp Pendleton and raised in Fontana, California. She was first professionally published in the Fontana Herald, in 1995 and worked for Fontana channel 3 as a camerawoman, director, and actress. Duran has performed in Grease and A Christmas Carol for Fontana City Mummers, was in Don't Drink the Water and Tartuffe for Fontana High School, and was an extra in Kazam (starring Shaquille O'neal) directed by Paul Michael Glaser.

Duran is currently the Guest Editor of *Boundless 2022*, of The Rio Grande Valley International Poetry Festival, DJ/Host for *The Collective* on KQBH LA 101.5 FM, the author of "*…and so, the Wind was Born,*" with

FlowerSong Press, and declared a Sapphic Author by *The Lesbian Review*. Duran is a Substitute teacher, Yoga Instructor, Massage Therapist, and an Art, Poetry, and Yoga teacher for the youth. She has taught workshops at Pitzer College, Chaffey College, Mt. SAC (Culturama), the University of Redlands, Joshua Home: an LGBTQ Youth Safe Haven, the Ontario TAY Center, and is a former Literary Director and Art Advocate for the dA: Center for the Arts. Duran has performed for the Autry Museum in LA (in the archived Herstory Mixed Tape exhibition), Chaffey College, Pitzer College, Life of JEM, Bridge the Gap, CMTY Live, Cafe con Libros, the American Poetry Museum, The Book Jewel, Centro Cultura de la Raza, LibroMobile, Tia Cuchas, The Village Well, and many more.

Duran has Associate of Arts degrees in Liberal Arts and Science and Studio Art from Chaffey College, Bachelor of Arts degrees in English and World Literature: Creative Writing and Studio Art from Pitzer College and is a VONA (Voices of Our Nation Artist Foundation) alumna. She is also the founder of the IE Hope Collective; an outreach that helps people living on the streets and in shelters, and provides poetry, art, and yoga workshops for low income, homeless, foster, refugee, and LGBTQ2+ youth (ages 7-18)——focusing on coping skills, empathy, introspection, mindfulness, and community building—which she developed during her time as a volunteer Community Health Worker for the San Bernardino County and from her studies in child development, psychology, criminal justice, and as a Summer Research Fellow at the University of Illinois Urbana-Champaign where she published her research titled *Sexual Violence and the Assimilation Response of LGBTQ2 Female Identified Latina and Indigenous Americans.*"

As an artist, poet, and educator: Duran plans to further her education in Art Therapy to aid marginalized youth.

Sin pan y sin trabajo

por Gabriel González Núñez

Poema ecfrástico a partir a de la
pintura homónima de Ernesto de la Cárcova

¿Qué busca la mirada del que está sin trabajo?
¿Qué fluye de los pechos de la que está sin pan?

¿Cómo llora el bebito del que está sin trabajo?
¿A qué suena el sollozo de la que está sin pan?

¿Qué se sirve en la mesa del que está sin trabajo?
¿Por qué cruje la silla de la que ésta sin pan?

¿Prenden la luz en casa del que está sin trabajo?
¿Desprende aroma el horno de la que está sin pan?

¿Por qué enmudece la voz del que está sin trabajo?
¿Por qué caen los hombros de la que está sin pan?

¿Para qué sirve el pico del que está sin trabajo?
¿A dónde va la rabia de la que está sin pan?

¿Qué sabor tiene el hambre sin pan y sin trabajo?
¿Qué sonido hace la sed sin pan y sin trabajo?
¿A qué huele el porvenir sin pan y sin trabajo?

Gabriel González Núñez es oriundo de Montevideo, Uruguay, y actualmente forma traductores en La Universidad de Texas en el Valle del Río Grande. Es autor del poemario *Ese golpe de luz* (FlowerSong Press 2020) y del plaquette digital *El ciclo / The Cycle* (Center for Latter-day Saint Arts 2020). También ha publicado poemas en revistas (p. ej., *The Chachalaca Review*) y antologías (p.ej. *El paso de los años*). Su poema "Un dios en quien confiar" formó parte del recital literario *Thorns & Thistles* (2019). Es autor también de diez libros para niños, todos ilustrados por Alicia Aguirre (Penguin Uruguay 2019, 2020, 2021, 2022). Asimismo es autor del libro de cuento *Rumbos* (Jade Publishing 2021). Además, con el cuento «Milonga del teatro» recibió mención de honor en el 36o. Concurso Dr. Alberto Manini Ríos y con «Anexo documental I» recibió mención de honor en el certamen Dándole la Vuelta al Mundo con la Literatura Mormona.

Beat, Meat, and Billionaires in Space
by Edward Vidaurre

The cow wants you to eat the meat
The goat, the chicken, the duck, the fish
All want you to eat
Chew slow and in silence

Even the horse
And the guinea pig, the armadillo
And the rat

The earth wants you to pull her hair
Grab her beets
The corn listens
and poets are still talking about
Kerouac and ginseng and Ginsberg
And the blues in Mexico City
But not about anything relevant to the blues in Mexico

Here is another beat poem, they say
up your alley! I say

I've been

Crying
                on the low
Hiding
                on the low
Healing
                on the low

I stopped listening to the tone in the poet's voice
I started listening to the words in the poet's song

I've been

Running
                in my dreams

Dying

        in yours

This liquid insomnia is a cutter
I have the scars to prove it
I have the dark circles under my eyes
My mouth turns into a candle wax grin
I try to yell but laughter fumbles between my teeth
Instead

I can't help but think of the dead
I watch movies and I'm reminded of

All the evil that lurks
Where is our savior? Their savior?

I've been

Praying
        For souls
Praying
        For numbers
Praying
        For answers

I dream of cows and billionaires
Cows in space
Billionaires between two buns
with lettuce, tomato, and onions
The cow wants me to eat the meat
Slow and in silence

Edward Vidaurre is an award-winning poet with eight collections of poetry, publisher and editor-in-chief of FlowerSong Press and Juventud Press. Editor of several anthologies and a 2022 inductee as a distinguished member of the Texas Institute of Letters.

Follow him on Twitter @VidaurreEdward and on Instagram @edward_vidaurre

FEATURED POETS

Featured Poet: Wang Ping

And the Birds Guide Us

A dewdrop hangs on the lip of an orchid
A volcano rumbles in another ether

Something has hit us
And we don't know why

It's April. The prairie
Is brewing a new blizzard

Cornfields adrift in the whiteout wind
One-legged cranes darken the braided river

Rings of ice like shackles
And the sky in an origami dream

At the fork of the road I stand in blindfold
Lines of hexagrams, form of the formless

This light and shadow-- it's all energy
Same difference in the field of perception
Every tomorrow has two handles
Every seed contains its own fortune

This is the truth to those who still trust
A thread so thin, unbreakable
Fire from the sea and into the sea—the Big
Island—ash from the womb of Earth

Children of the rivers and mountains
We carry a dream as ancient as the cranes

Sailing across the sky, ocean and desert
Uttering a cry that's almost too human

The birds have moved on
And the fields still aquiver with their spirits

They do not think   they live
Simply   each day a small gift

The River Has No Tongue

A starving waif pulses from the window screen
Wei cries his heart out for his stolen I-phone
My fingers type out thoughts filling the air with pellets of rain
Across the river, a lover cuts open a bleeding orange

At the window my face opens to the mid-winter sun
Heavy doses of Vitamin D to calm inflamed keloids
The Mississippi is half frozen half open
Dogs and skiers move on the ice with a heart-wrenching grace

We seek fire to ignite the universe
We summon darkness to fight demons
The rivers meet and curve around the bend
Our paths crisscross, but never touch

Deep in the snow, trees stand naked
A silent vow unleashes its wings
Who says memory has no soul?
See how it extends its roots, bone to bone

A woodpecker calls from the abandoned tepee
A lotus blooms through the mirror of ice
The river has no tongue
Fish and turtles roam with raven spirits

Confession of Ruby-throat

in China, xiao xin 小心 is for caution
the heart gets smaller with each step of
hesitation, the shell of xin shrunken with fear
小心—a shriveled heart spilling blood

xiao xin—blue whale's car-sized heart
pumping 10 tons of blood
through its 200-ton body

yet the heart champion belongs to us
beating 1200 per minute in our chest
a body lighter than ten pinto beans
wings and tail screeching with joy
as we dive for our beloved
neon feathers lighting the air

there's no other way to love
the monster rumbles in lower fields, his lava
breaths melting hesitant feet along the path
be careful, cries the mother
to her child tumbling forward
pulling ropes tied to his waist
xiao xin: to become small
and smaller with each step
how does a fledgling enter the sky with a fearful heart?
how do we fly without tumbling first, head to the earth?
how do we live without knowing the taste of dying
each night, our heart slows to a halt
our being, lighter than a penny, half filled with sugar
the other half offered to the night's lord
oh, how can we have regrets: to die each night
for tomorrow's feast, an orgy of flight and nectar--

there's no other way to live
even if it means forever on the edge of starving
to dive into 1500 flowers daily, to cross the Gulf

with a day's food, to be alive breathlessly
wings beating 200 a second, heart firing
600 a minute at rest, and doubling for a flight--

there's no other way to cross
from Mexico to Alaska, our 2-gram body
full with nectar, the rest is our heart--enormous
thrown into the wind, into the unknown
xiao xin--courage is not an absence of fear
the secret lies in our willingness to live
hours away from death, each night
in torpor, losing half of our being
as we cross seas and deserts
falling out of the sky
uttering cries half human half beast

Ode to Virus

Our cell is a hundred times bigger
Our body? Ten million larger!
But why are we so terrified of you
Quantum buggers on earth?
You're so puny, 50 millions of you in a teaspoon
of water, and 500 millions on a pinpoint

Is it because you outnumber all life together
On earth, ten million more than all the stars in space?
Because you live on the edge of life
As a hijacker, parasite, cuckoo, vine
Clinging, copying, sucking life out of your hosts
Turning us into your slaves, zombies, mutants?

Or because life is impossible without you:
No bacteria, cells or trees, no brains or civilization?
Because 8 % of you are buried deep in our genomes
As provirus, as our core makeups of DNA
Jumpstarting our T cells to fend off invaders?
When we get sick, it means you, provirus
Is dozing off, taking a break?

Because you spread like metaphors, defying space, time and logic
Quantum leaps from bacteria to bacteria, mosquito to mosquito
Through saliva, tears, sweat, mucus, blood, skin
Bird to bird, bat to bat, human to human?
Or a tossup between bat to bird, bird to swine, swine to human…
As flu, polio, small pox, herpes, AIDS, Zika, rabies, Ebola, SARS, Covid-19…
Turning the world into a Zombie land?

Because you suck our blood and steal our cells,
Then mutate our genes into cancer
Or turn starch and fat into your food, so we get fed too?
Is that why you kill us and keep us alive at the same time
Building our immunity, then making us ill so we get stronger?
Are you biological pumps to jolt life, accelerate decay?
Without you, we'd be buried under debris, bodies, woods?

So quantum buggers from cosmos?
Should I hate you or love you or both?
I want to expel you but I need you to live
I need to kill you, but killing you also kills me
because I'm part of you!
You're Vampire of the Earth!
The most terrifying, most beautiful in your crowns
With your efficiency, guile, intelligence!

Ultra vires, power beyond law and logic
You are not alive, yet live everywhere!
You're our enigma, our karma
You're the poison we have to live with and can't live without
In fact poison is your Latin name
Chinese made it even worse: bingdu--病毒--diseased virus

Is that why you gave us Spanish Flu, SARS, Swine, Bird?
Or you're just being you, a trickster, a teacher and master
Showing us how to respect all sentient being on the planet
Including you, Corona, the only way to handle you
Is to embrace you, the way we keep our enemy close
Building up our pro-viruses so that bad ones can't occupy?
Is immunity nothing but billions of you negotiating
Space in our body, on the planet?
Is this another word for Balance, equilibrium, co-habitat?
Is this your equation of Life=Love2?

15TH ANNUAL

V.I.P.F.
RIO GRANDE VALLEY
INTERNATIONAL POETRY FESTIVA
WWW.VALLEYPOETRYFEST.ORG

15TH ANNUAL

V.I.P.F.
RIO GRANDE VALLEY
INTERNATIONAL POETRY FESTIVA
WWW.VALLEYPOETRYFEST.ORG

www.valleypoetryfest.org

Featured Poet: Wang Ping was born in Shanghai and came to the USA in 1986. She is the founder and director of the Kinship of Rivers project, an international project that builds kinship among the people who live along the Mississippi, Yangtze, Ganges, Amazons, Nile Rivers through exchanging gifts of art, poetry, stories, music, dance and food. She has paddled many rivers and their tributaries, giving poetry and art workshops along the river communities, making thousands of flags as gifts and peace ambassadors between the Mississippi and the Yangtze Rivers.

Her publications include *My Name Is Immigrant, poetry,* Hang Loose Press 2020, *Life of Miracles along the Yangtze and Mississippi,* AWP creative non-fiction award, University of Georgia Press 2018, *Ten Thousand Waves,* poetry from Wings Press, 2014, *American Visa* (short stories, 1994), *Foreign Devil* (novel, 1996), *Of Flesh and Spirit* (poetry, 1998), *The Magic Whip* (poetry, 2003), *The Last Communist Virgin* (stories, 2007), all from Coffee House, *New Generation: Poetry from China Today,*

1999 from Hanging Loose Press, *Flash Cards: Poems by Yu Jian,* co-translation with Ron Padgett, 2010 from Zephyr Press. *Aching for Beauty: Footbinding in China* (2000, University of Minnesota Press, 2002 paperback by Random House) won the Eugene Kayden Award for the Best Book in Humanities. *The Last Communist Virgin* won the 2008 Minnesota Book Award and Asian American Studies Award.

Her new poetry book *My Name Is Immigrant,* is long listed for the National Book Award, Critic Circuit Book award, Pen Literary Award, Griffin International Poetry Award, among many others.

She had many multimedia solo exhibitions: "We Are Water: Kinship of Rivers" a one-month exhibition that brought 100 artists from the Yangtze and Mississippi Rivers to celebrate water (Soap Factory, 2014), "Behind the Gate: After the Flooding of the Three Gorges" at Janet Fine Art Gallery(2007), "All Roads to Lhasa" at Banfill-Locke Cultural Center(2008), "Kinship of Rivers" at the Soap Factory(2011, 12), Great River Museum in Illinois(2012), Fireworks Press at St. Louis(2012), Great River Road Center at Prescott (2012), Wisconsin, Emily Carr University in Vancouver(2013), University of California Santa Barbara(2013), and many other places.

She collaborated with the British filmmaker Isaac Julien on *Ten Thousand Waves,* a film installation about the illegal Chinese immigration in London, the composer and musician Bruce Bolon, Alex Wand (Grammy award winner), Gao Hong, etc..

She is the recipient of National Endowment for the Arts, New York Foundation for the Arts, New York State Council of the Arts, Minnesota State Arts Board, the Bush Artist Fellowship, Lannan Foundation Fellowship, Vermont Studio Center Fellowship, and the McKnight Artist Fellowship. She received her Distinct Immigrant Award in 2014, and Venezuela International Poet of Honor in 2015.

Wang Ping taught creative writing as Professor of English at Macalester College for 21 years, and is now a Professor Emerita.

www.wangping.com
www.behindthegateexhibit.wangping.com
www.kinshipofrivers.org

FEATURED POET: DENISE CHÁVEZ

Mop/Trapeador

How hard can it be to find a mop in Las Cruces, New Mexico?
42 miles from the U.S./Mexico border
Give it a try, Mi Gente

You'll find a mop near the front door
In My Mexicano part of town
My Camino Real side of town
My Jornada del Muerte side of town
My Poor Eastside full of crumbling adobes, bad plaster jobs, dilapidated abandoned cars, aging saggy couches dumped curbside
Random reckless dogs walking nonchalantly mid-street without a care in the world side of town
Streets with names like Tornillo, Mesquite, Espina
Streets named for trees and goat heads and Western states

Oh, you'll find that mop alright Outside the houses of Mi Gente
That upended old mop near their front door drying out in the sun
No moisture to be accounted for no matter the season
Our mops are always dry

What do our mops say to the passerby?
Their grey, over-washed greñas upside down near too many front doors?

111

We clean
We are a cleaning people
We're too busy cleaning your home to clean ours
We work hard
But not hard enough to make a decent living
We can't afford that fancy $199 Steam Mop on Sale at Best Buy

We're in a hurry
There's always something else to attend to
Children, animals, family

It's not that we're afraid of mops, no
Not on this side of town
Not Mi Gente Function rules here
Trapo rag side flailing out
A cotton crown for all to see
Long hairy strands dried out and shaped by wind and sand
The old kind with the long cotton grey entrails

The old mops we knew were wrung out by hand
Remember them?
That twisting turning motion of hands
The old tina full of brownish water
An ugly chore now your turn

We know the old trapeador
We've danced with it, swabbed, soaked it, splattered, sprayed with it, laid it down, picked it up
again and again
We've all taken a turn with La Greñuda.

The mop from the grocery store with a retractable head
Gave way to the steam mop
It was a good idea, Carnala,
Because it's YOU I'm addressing you, the woman who mops
Let me ask you: when was the last time you saw a man in your family use a trapeador?
A fregadora? El lampazo.. El Trapero. El Mapo. La Mopa. El Mopeador. El Mechudo.
La Greña. Los Fregasuelos. El Piso Fregona

The steam mop was a good idea until the manufacturer did away with that model
And stopped making the $7 soap you had to buy at that special store

112

I am back to the blue headed mop
I refuse to go back to the trapeador
They were good in their way
They swabbed a good swatch

We saw our mothers and our mother's helpers
Ayudantes, not maids, use them
We saw them drag that mop head like a ball and chain across that familiar floor
Exhausted they were and still working
Someone always had to get down on their hands and knees to get those corners

Now that I am older—I can get down now
It's the getting up that is the harder part
I can back down a flight of stairs
It's the going forward that strains

Mi Gente
You with the mops near your front door
What would it take to bring them inside?
Leave them out back?
Tucked in a corner of the kitchen?
In that utility room?
In the garage?
Away from the light of day
From the peering eyes of those who drive by and wonder
Why the hell are there so many mops by the door in this neighborhood?

My side of town
Is now giving way to gentrification
Sad to see, Mi Gente,
You don't see our mops there in those new stuccoed houses, do you?
Those remodels EVERYONE but Mi Gente is going to make money from
You'll never see them inside or outside
Not those old raggedy-assed mop heads waving in the April wind
Like unkempt moco-nosed chamacos with lagaña-crusted eyes
Saying to all the world
Somos Mexicanos
Somos Chicanas
I live here and so does my mop
Unos de esos

Fellos
Viejitos
Pelludos
Lleno de no se que y más
Yeah, that kind of mop
The old ones

Once a neighbor in Santa Fe – a skinny white guy whose name I don't care to remember—tried
to borrow my mop.
"I'll bring it right back
Hell no, hell no!
¡Cómo que?
Don't you NEVER EVER lend a mop out to anyone!
How dare you?
A mop is sacred
Don't you know that Cabrón?
A mop is sacred!

My mop stories are full of my mother's helpers
Their names resonate in my mind and I remember them all:
Cata, Ninfa, Belsora, Isa, Lina, any number of Maria's
They knew mops

I once got a job cleaning a house
I lasted one week
One pasada of a young teacher friend of my mother, a woman's not-too-dirty house
and that was it
I couldn't take it

I have great respect for those who clean and mop
Moping takes stamina and time.
A commitment
To mop or not to mop?
That is the question?

My steam mop is dead
Out of commission
Outdated
A dinosaur of the mopping kind
No soap available anywhere

I called the company
No supervisor on hand to listen to complaints
That poor woman in India answering just another call
From someone complaining about a mop halfway across the world

Just how hard it is to find a good mop in my hometown?
Lard I can understand at Christmastime for those biscochos
Corn husks for those tamales
Green chile at the end of the season
But a mop?

I am mop-less
Memories of mops swirling around
Memories of all the women in my life
Mopping and working and bending to get into those corners
agachando porque era necesario
It was necessary to get those corners
To get the job done
Not only done
But Well done

¡Caray! Mi Gente!
What do mops by the front door say about us?

Put away your hair shirt

Take off your crown of thorns
You don't need to be the Savior of the World
All you need to do is show up
Be present
This is how we process the world's suffering
Sitting
Observing
How alike we are

Beautiful girls stop showing us your breasts
We see them
Let your passion rest
Someday, you too, will get old
My mother once told me that
I remember her words

Fathers, stop talking about your fame, your conquests, your success
The places in the world you've traveled and what you have done
Without taking a breath you tell about your son
how many times he's been shot, stabbed, run over, almost killed, and how he is
now living in a homeless shelter
You never gave me his name
Listen to yourself
Your foolishness
You've taught him certain things, but not to love

Writers, stop telling us how great your book is
And what a gift to the world it is
And how much it means to you to someone
to anyone
We know
Take up your pen again
Tell us the story of how the world goes on
And on

Tell me the story of that young man

That one young man
Who kept coming back
And back again
Into that room
Because he had to
Something in that room was waiting for him
Calling him
He was looking for something
What was it?

Stop now.
Process the Suffering
We are in the Confessional
Let us tell each other our sins

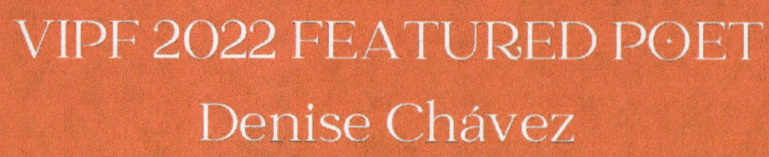

VIPF 2022 FEATURED POET
Denise Chávez

15TH ANNUAL

V.I.P.F.

RIO GRANDE VALLEY
INTERNATIONAL POETRY FESTIVAL
WWW.VALLEYPOETRYFEST.ORG

15TH ANNUAL

V.I.P.F

RIO GRANDE VALLEY
INTERNATIONAL POETRY FESTI
WWW.VALLEYPOETRYFEST.ORG

www.valleypoetryfest.org

Denise Chávez is the author of *The King and Queen of Comezón, Loving Pedro Infante, A Taco Testimony: Meditations on Family, Food and Culture* and *Face of An Angel*, among other works. Chávez is the Co-Founder, with Kari Lenander, Executive Director of The Border Servant Corps (BSC) of Libros Para El Viaje, an ongoing Refugee, Migrant, and Asylum-seeker book gathering and distribution initiative that delivers books to children and families on the U.S./Mexico border in collaboration with The Border Servant Corps.

Currently Chavez is co-editing, with Dr. Enrique Lamadrid, former Head of Chicano/Latino programs at the University of New Mexico, an upcoming anthology *WE ARE HERE TO REPRESENT*, which will feature the work of multi-generational writers and artists telling the story of their service to Refugee and Migrant families.

For more information on Libros Para El Viaje: https://www.borderservantcorps. org/libros-para-el-viaje

Featured Poet: Roberto Carlos Garcia

To write a poem

you must seek a beautiful moment,
at least one a day, so I hug
the Japanese Maple—force the issue;
play the fable out & go deeper into the woods
in search of what to love
but the Twisted Orange Tree is spikey & low
to the ground so I kneel because sometimes
its ok to grovel for a taste of that sweet
thing you're begging after; if it could my need
would burst—a Flowering Dogwood—or soak up
rainy day mist like Kentucky Coffeetrees,
here I am though, staring in the wooded mirror house
of a Bald Cypress; the ground turns from leaf dust
to moss & mold & the greener grass of dissatisfaction
lies dormant, Common Persimmons perfume the air
Red Horsechestnuts lob shadows & hold the chill
while I pass the tulips into a circle of Black Gum trees small
enough to climb, wide enough to hide in; there I stare
at this beautiful moment for as long as I can

Featured Poet: Roberto Carlos Garcia - Poet, storyteller, and essayist Roberto Carlos Garcia is a self-described "sancocho […] of provisions from the Harlem Renaissance, the Spanish Poets of 1929, the Black Arts Movement, the Nuyorican School, and the Modernists." Garcia is rigorously interrogative of himself and the world around him, conveying "nakedness of emotion, intent, and experience," and he writes extensively about the Afro-Latinx and Afro-diasporic experience. Roberto's third collection, *[Elegies]*, is published by Flower Song Press and his second poetry collection, *black / Maybe: An Afro Lyric*, is available from Willow Books. Roberto's first collection, *Melancolía*, is available from Červená Barva Press.

His poems and prose have appeared or are forthcoming in POETRY Magazine, *The BreakBeat Poets Vol 4: LatiNEXT, Bettering American Poetry Vol. 3, The Root, Those People, Rigorous, Academy of American Poets Poem-A-Day, Gawker, Barrelhouse, The Acentos Review, Lunch Ticket*, and many others.

He is founder of the cooperative press Get Fresh Books Publishing, A NonProfit Corp.

A native New Yorker, Roberto holds an MFA in Poetry and Poetry in Translation from Drew University, and has been nominated for a Pushcart Prize.

Featured Poet: Benito Pastoriza Iyodo

El peligro de la noche violada

Todos los cantos han conocido tu voz
palabra del pecho generado
en vidas tatuadas de placer

eres el peligro de la noche violada
la tortura de la esquina escondida
el sentimiento de las lápidas contempladas

con tanta furia enredada de subsuelos sexuales
con tantos ecos rojos perforados

en mañanas de silencios y éxtasis
en noches de sudores y llantos
en tardes de cuevas encendidas

por esta amenazada furia de amor
por este homicidio de la fuerza entregada
por lo causante que queda repetido

desde esta parte de lo deshecho
desde el contorno de lo amamantado
desde este rendimiento que no espera

a esta voz que se ahoga en el pecho
a este tacto del dolor que conoce

los plomos encadenados
las trenzas de los cuerpos arropados

para no sentir el regreso
para quedarse en la espera

del minuto en torbellinos
porque ha sido la muerte de la piel
la vida
del homicidio en el amor

The danger of the violated night

translation by Bradley Warren Davis

All of the chants have known your voice
word of the chest generated
in lives tattooed by pleasure

you are the danger of the violated night
the torture of the hidden corner
the sentiment of contemplated tombstones

with so much wrath tangled in the sexual undergrounds
with so many red perforated echoes

in mornings of silences and ecstasies
in nights of sweats and whimpers
in afternoons of burning caves

by this threatened fury of love
by that homicide of surrendered strength
by the cause that's still repeated

from this part of what's undone
from the outline of the suckled
from this performance which does not wait

to this voice that drowns in the chest
to that touch of pain that knows

the chained lead
the braids of bodies covered

so as not to feel the return
to remain in waiting

of the minute in whirlwinds
because it has been death
of the flesh
the life
of homicide in love

Las puertas giratorias

hoy te sueño en las esquinas
en los bulevares de la transparencia
en los recovecos de las memorias grises
donde Tenochtitlán se confunde con Uxmal
cuando salgo por la puerta de Alcalá en Madrid
pero no te encuentro te has perdido como siempre
en la Plaza de la Independencia que se comunica con el Patio
de los Leones en Granada donde te has vuelto a perder querido

y llego hasta Buenos Aires
esperándote frente al Teatro Colón
y tú estás en Guayaquil paseándote junto
al río Guayas esperándome cerca del Hemiciclo
de la Rotunda donde Simón Bolívar y San Martín
se dan la mano pero yo estoy en el otro malecón el
de La Habana donde me cuelo por las puertas de la Catedral
de la Concepción Inmaculada pero tú me estabas esperando en

la Primada de América en la calle Isabel La Católica
salgo por la puerta y casi te alcanzo a la entrada de Machu Picchu
donde reapareces frente a la Puerta de San Juan donde miras atontado la bahía
y los fuertes te dije que me esperaras en la Caída del Ángel en el parque Canaima
pero tú perdido en Antigua en Tegucigalpa perdido en la casa de Neruda
revelar este amor que se me escapa por las salidas por las puertas del olvido
una queda abierta otra queda cerrada y allí quedaremos con las manos extendidas
procurando reinventar este sentimiento en las páginas giratorias de la historia

The revolving doors

translation by Bradley Warren Davis

Today I dream of you on the corners
on the boulevards of transparency
in the recesses of gray memories
where Tenochtitlan is confused with Uxmal
when I leave through the gate of Alcala in Madrid
but I cannot find you you've gotten lost as always
in Independence Square that connects with the Court
of the Lions in Granada where you've again gotten lost love

and I arrive to Buenos Aires
waiting for you in front of Teatro Colon
and you are in Guayaquil strolling along
the Guayas River awaiting me near the semicircle
of the Rotunda where Simon Bolívar and San Martin
shake hands but I am in the other esplanade the one
in Havana where I slip through the doors of the Cathedral
of the Immaculate Conception but you were waiting for me in

the First Cathedral of the Americas on Isabel La Católica Street
I exit the door and I almost catch you at the entrance to Machu Picchu
where you reappear in front of the San Juan Gate where you look dazed at the bay
and the fortresses I told you to wait for me at Angel Falls in Canaima Park
but you lost in Antigua in Tegucigalpa lost in the house of Neruda
to reveal this love that escapes me through the exits through the doors of forgetfulness
one stays open another stays closed and there we will remain with our hands extended
seeking to reinvent this sentiment on the revolving pages of history

sangre en las manos

desde el momento en que dijiste mira ese marica
mira ese maricón joto pato plumífero puto putete

cuando señalaste con tus cinco dedos de verdugo
aquel que tanto odias aquel que tanto desprecias

en el preciso momento de persignarte tres veces
porque supuestamente pedías bendita absolución

para el pobre amanerado el sodomita el invertido
te acuerdas el día el mes la fecha en que le negaste

el empleo el puesto la oportunidad de la promoción
es afeminado marica mala imagen para la compañía

las patadas las palizas las puñaladas los parricidios
linchamientos ejecuciones ahorcamientos asesinatos

en el medio oriente en **áfrica honduras** jamaica rusia
en el exótico brasil se asesina uno cada veintiocho horas

en madrid a palizas cada vez que al macho le dé la gana
en san juan le harán la vida imposible porque eres escoria

y tú sin denunciar los ojos tapados con oídos sordos
eso les pasa por ser maricones jotos quien les manda

sí aquel fue el momento clave el preciso instante tuyo
cuando te volviste cómplice ejecutor asesino monstruo

porque ahora llevabas sangre en las manos esa terrible
sangre que no se limpia ni se borra sangre de asesino

blood on your hands
translation by Bradley Warren Davis

from the moment you said look at that sissy
look at that fag queer fairy queen faggot homo

when you pointed out with your five tormentor's fingers
that which you so hate that which you despise so much

in the precise moment of crossing yourself three times
because supposedly you had asked for blessed absolution

for the poor effeminate the sodomite the homo
you remember the day the month the date in which you denied it

the job the position the opportunity of a promotion
he's an effeminate fag a bad image for the company

the kickings the beatings the stabbings the parricides
lynchings executions hangings murders

in the middle east in africa honduras jamaica russia
in exotic brazil one is murdered every twenty-four hours

in madrid by beatings whenever some macho wants to
in san juan they will make your life impossible because you are scum

and you without denouncing it eyes covered with deaf ears
that's what happens for being fags queers who makes them do it

yes that was the key moment the precise instant for you
when you became accomplice executioner murderer monster

because now you wear blood on your hands that terrible
blood that won't wash off nor fade blood of an assassin

Benito Pastoriza Iyodo is an author of poetry, poetics, fiction and literary articles. The themes of his literary works include: man's evolution from childhood to adulthood, examination of self, the precipices of culture and its rituals, violence in the cities, examination of stereotypes, the constructs of communication, gender roles and sexuality, education systems and racism, exploitation and the manifestation of exclusion through political and economic powers.

His literary career is manifested in eight books: five collections of poetry, a novel and two books of short stories. Three books of poetry and one volume of short stories have been published in bilingual editions (the original Spanish and English). The author's poems and short stories have been included in anthologies and journals published in the United States, Latin America and Spain.

His published works are: *The color of the colorless (Lo coloro de lo incoloro)*, *A matter of men (Cuestión de hombres)*, *September Elegies (Elegías de septiembre)*, *Letters to the shadow of your love (Cartas a la sombra de tu piel)*, *The waters of Paradise (El agua del paraíso)*, *Beloved, beloved of my heart (Nena, nena de mi corazón)*, *Brothel of the word (Prostíbulo de la palabra)* and *Hominis Aurora*.

Benito Pastoriza Iyodo was born in Puerto Rico. He received his bachelor's degree in English and Hispanic Studies at the University of Puerto Rico. Later, he obtained his master's degree in Spanish Language and Literature at the University of California, Santa Barbara. He completed his doctoral coursework in Romance Languages and Literatures at the University of Chicago.

He has been recognized through various literary prizes, including the Ateneo Puertorriqueño Prize, the Chicano/Latino Literary Prize, the Julio Cortázar Prize (Uruguay) and the Hispanic Culture Review Poetry Award.

Featured Poet: Xánath Caraza

Niña sin nombre

Golpe certero
en el pecho

una víctima más,
niña sin nombre.

¡Hijas arrebatadas
de los caminos!

Gimes en la
penumbra

por el abuso
de tu cuerpo.

Niña sin nombre
en las calles adoquinadas.

La inocencia
fue lluvia.

Tu carne lacerada
por el viento.

Tus entrañas
desgarradas.

¿Quién impide hacerte justicia?
¿Quién impide tu curación?

Se escurren las
silenciosas lágrimas
de sangre.

Se desbordan
los ríos
color carmín.

¡Cubren las calles!

¡Cuántas anónimas voces!

Girl with No Name

translation by Sandra Kingery

Direct blow
to the chest

one more victim,
girl with no name.

Daughters snatched
off the streets!

You moan in
the shadows

your body
abused.

Girl with no name
on cobblestoned corners.

Innocence
became rain.

Your flesh slashed
by wind.

Your entrails
torn asunder.

Who stops justice?
Who stops your healing?

Silent tears
of blood
seeping down.

Carmine colored

rivers
slip their banks.

They fill the streets!

So many anonymous voices!

9.

Es el dolor de un pueblo
el que **se desliza** en
la sangre de la tierra.

Acantilados bermejos
contienen **la angustia**
y las rítmicas palpitaciones.

La gente murmura en las
doradas esquinas de la ciudad,
se desliza la esperanza
con sutileza acuática.

¿dónde están los héroes del agua?
¿dónde las mujeres pez que **cantan en la aurora**?
¿dónde las ilusiones del nuevo amanecer?

Todo se inunda.

Escurre **la lluvia**
en los cristales,
de los acantilados
brota el agua densa.

Canta, mujer pez, canta.

9.

translation by Sandra Kingery

It is the people's pain
sneaking into
the blood of the land.

Crimson cliffs
contain the **anguish**
and rhythmic palpitations.

People murmur in the
golden corners of the city,
hope slips away
with aquatic subtlety.

where are the heroes of the water?
where the fish women and their **song of first light**?
where the illusions of the new dawn?

Everything becomes flooded.

Rain drips
down window panes,
dense water
sprouts from cliffs.

Sing, fish woman, sing.

VIPF 2022 FEATURED POET
Xánath Caraza

15TH ANNUAL

V.I.P.F.
RIO GRANDE VALLEY
INTERNATIONAL POETRY FESTIVA
WWW.VALLEYPOETRYFEST.ORG

15TH ANNUAL

V.I.P.F.
RIO GRANDE VALLEY
INTERNATIONAL POETRY FESTIVA
WWW.VALLEYPOETRYFEST.ORG

www.valleypoetryfest.org

Xánath Caraza is a traveler, educator, poet, short story writer, and translator. She writes for *La Bloga, Revista Literaria Monolito,* and *Seattle Escribe.* In 2021 *It Pierces the Skin* received Bronze Medal for the Juan Felipe Herrera Best Book of Poetry. In 2020 *Balamkú* received second place for the Juan Felipe Herrera Best Book of Poetry Award. In 2019 for the International Latino Book Awards she received Second Place for *Hudson* for "Best Book of Poetry in Spanish" and Second Place for *Metztli* for Best Short Story Collection. In 2018 for the International Latino Book Awards she received First Place for *Lágrima* roja for "Best Book of Poetry in Spanish by One Author" and First Place for *Sin preámbulos / Without Preamble* for "Best Book of Bilingual Poetry". Her book of poetry *Syllables of Wind / Sílabas de viento* received the 2015 International Book Award for Poetry. She was Writer-in-Residence at Westchester Community College, NY, 2016-2019. Caraza was the recipient of the 2014 Beca Nebrija para Creadores, Universidad de Alcalá de Henares in Spain. She was named number one of the 2013 Top Ten Latino Authors by LatinoStories.com. Her books of verse *Where the Light is Violet, Black Ink, Ocelocíhuatl, Conjuro* and her book of short fiction *What the Tide Brings* have won national and international recognition. Her other books of poetry are *Fără* *preambul,* Μαύρη μελάνη, *Le sillabe del vento, Noche de colibríes,* and *Corazón pintado.* Caraza has been translated into English, Italian, Romanian, and Greek; and partially translated into Nahuatl, Portuguese, Hindi, and Turkish. Her new book of poetry is titled *Jackeline's Butterfly* (FlowerSong Press, 2022).

POEMAS SELECCIONADOS Y EDITADOS POR GABRIEL GONZÁLEZ NÚÑEZ

¿Qué esconderá?

por Érika Elisa Garza Tamez

Tal vez piojos viajeros
o *maybe* un mes de mucho sueño.
Quizás mil miedos
o ilusiones únicas inspiradas en el cielo.

¿Me esconderá sonrisas?
¿O estará chimuelo?
¿Esconderá palabras bonitas?
¿O en secreto querrá ser abuelo?

Es posible que tenga espías escondidos
esperando encontrar el amor verdadero
o enamorado esté de amores prohibidos.
¿Acaso esconderá un corazón sincero?

Posiblemente esconda secretos,
puede que sus sentimientos.
A lo mejor guarda millones de versos
escondidos bajo esos cabellos.

Erika Elisa Garza Tamez is a performer, poet and Spanish professor with STC. She holds a masters of arts in Spanish from UTRGV. Her poetry has been published in over 10 anthologies and magazines including *Boundless 2019-2020*. She recently published her poetry collection "Con alas de mariposa."

A partir de mañana, todo
por Ana Karen Degollado

Esto ocurrirá
según creo, en plena

oscuridad

¿está todo preparado
para nosotros?

lento y desparramado cordero
no muerdas
una plegaria cada vez
frente a ti, prometo

ciega por el humo
una fiesta
                    para ti

sal amarga, consagrada

sobre las petrificaciones
las líneas indivisibles
y los vientos

dicen que no hay silencio

con el que debas acercarte
a este dios,
nada que impida realizar este sacrificio
tan pronto llegues

¿qué deuda tengo yo?

llevo, lavo y despedazo
las entrañas, el tiempo
lo amaso sosteniendo un pan

sacando
el cántaro del pozo
animales que muerden y atacan

a escondidas
inoportuna

Yo no quería todo para mí.

Ana Karen Degollado -Poet born in Mexico City, but a nomad almost all her life. She studied philosophy and anthropology. She writes about cinema, ghosts, the desert and the impossible. She is part of the editorial committee of the digital magazine *Verité*. She is part of the 2022 generation of the literary residency *Under the volcano*, held in Tepoztlán, Morelos.

As of tomorrow, everything
por Ana Karen Degollado

This will happen

I believe, in full

darkness
is everything ready
for us?

slow and scattered lamb
don't bite
a prayer at a time
in front of you, I promise

blinded by smoke
a feast

                    for you

consecrated, bitter salt,

on the petrifactions
the indivisible lines
and the winds

they say there is no silence

with which you should approach
this god,
nothing to keep you from
making this sacrifice
as soon as you arrive

what debt do I owe?

I carry, wash and tear apart

the entrails, I knead time
holding a loaf of bread pulling
the pitcher from the well
animals that bite and attack

secretly
untimely

I did not want it all for me.

Ana Karen Degollado -Poet born in Mexico City, but a nomad almost all her life. She studied philosophy and anthropology. She writes about cinema, ghosts, the desert and the impossible. She is part of the editorial committee of the digital magazine *Verité*. She is part of the 2022 generation of the literary residency *Under the volcano*, held in Tepoztlán, Morelos.

95 % del universo

por Uriel Hernández Gonzaga

A veces imagino que estoy en los 90 y somos aquello que odiamos.
Aquello que besamos por las noches.
Esa falta de oxígeno.
Esa presencia de polvo cósmico en nuestra habitación donde evolucionan seres líquidos.
Donde las ventanas crujen y lloran.
Somos algo impreciso.
Somos algo impreciso y diminuto.
Me suspendo.
Tengo una imagen de ti en 3D.
Tengo una imagen de ti en 3D y la beso para fugarme.

Uriel Hernández Gonzaga (Aguas Blancas, Gro – México, 1992). Es psicólogo, poeta y artista visual. Poemas y cuentos suyos han sido publicados en diversas revistas digitales e impresas. Ganador del concurso Día del escritor, Bruma Ediciones, Argentina. Su trabajo ha sido incluido en la Antología Homenaje a Antonio Machado, editorial Artgerust, Madrid, España. Antología de cuento Red de Letras, antología de escritores acapulqueños. Antología Poética Migraciones. Ed. ABN Arte Buhonero, Tijuana B.C, México, Antología para el Festival Hello Melbourne, Revarena Ediciones y a Voz Limpia, Australia, entre otras. Actualmente se dedica a la divulgación de la ciencia y colabora en espacios destinados a la poesía experimental.

Un nombre plural

por Sandra Dolores Gómez-Amador

Me llamas por un nombre que no es el mío porque en este cuerpo tengo
grabada la violencia entre la que creció la abuela.
Me la heredó como quien hereda ojos verdes, cabello quebradizo o un
lunar en el muslo derecho.

Tengo marcadas sus historias de la niñez:
una camioneta con cuarenta cuerpos en ella, un bosque
talado para que las mujeres no fingieran ser árboles, para que no se
escondieran por las noches: un pacto de silencio no dicho.
En este cuerpo cargo con una guerra a la mitad:
guerra no triunfada,
      guerra no declarada,
            guerra jamás terminada.

Me llamas por un nombre que no es el mío
porque en este país no hay nombres propios,
comparto el nombre de mi abuela y de todas sus muertes;
el de todas las que fueron halcones y después nada.

En mi cuerpo ves sus rostros y en el suyo los nuestros. Nos llamas por otro nombre que no
nos pertenece porque no sabes cómo llamarnos. Tenemos un nombre plural, uno
impronunciable: nosotras.

Sandra Dolores Gómez-Amador - Poet, writer, and researcher. English
major at Universidad Nacional Autónoma de México. Co-founder of
Red Universitaria de Mujeres Escritoras. Her work has been published in
both online and print media.

La ceremonia

por Fátima Alvarado

Estaban los platos puestos en la mesa,
había también servilletas decoradas,
vasos que centelleaban llenos de sangría y en el centro un ramo de florecillas.

El cielo se teñía de magenta con detestable crudeza como sabiendo lo que pasaría;
el final de nuestras fechas más adoradas.

Los domesticados se volvieron fierecillas.

Entre la exacerbación se acercaba el precipicio que siendo exactos llegó fútil y sin
fundamento, pero estaba allí, una predicción pretérita
que, a juzgar por el momento, llegaba certera.

Era nuestra ceremonia, la ceremonia,
con ella carecían impasibles nuestros tiempos felices sin que existiera entre ellos otra
imposición más que la de salir de allí, salvajemente y sin regreso.

Fátima Alvarado, escritora y politóloga mexicana. En 2015 colaboró en la escritura de un libro antológico de poesía escolar. Ha colaborado en plataformas de escritura como la Red Universitaria de Mujeres Escritoras. Ha realizado investigaciones en torno a la violencia política de género. Interesada en la poesía, narrativa y ensayo.

Las cosas bellas

por Eneida Alcalde

Un vestido tejido a mano,
rojo y único como tu voz.

Una madre que se corta las uñas
día tras día y prepara leche, siempre tibia,
y te acurruca murmurando te quiero
sabionda, traviesa siempre
lista como mis padres
logrando sus sueños en un país ajeno
que nunca supo lo que hacer con sus nombres largos
que nunca encajaron en sus cajas
fabricadas por un sistema
que nunca paró obsesionando
con la blancura de su piel.

Porque la vida es así nena,
roja y profunda igual a tus labios
sonriendo hacia el futuro
a pesar de tantas millas lejos
de los que nunca te quisieron y
los que te siguen queriendo
mientras la vida pasa
todo pasa por
manos migratorias
forjando este mundo
a través de las épocas
puntada a puntada
como el vestido rojo,
no hay otro.

No hay otro.

Eneida Alcalde immigrated to the United States as a child, transplanting her Chilean-Puerto Rican roots into Pennsylvanian soil. Her background fuels her poetry, which seeks to ask questions, explore mysteries, and elevate the underrepresented. Recent publications include poems in *riverSedge*, *Two Hawks Quarterly*, and *Magma Poetry*. Learn more at www.eneidaescribe.com.

razón de ser

por Gustavo Gac-Artigas

¿cuál es el sentido de mis versos?
pregunté

el viento
misericordioso
dio vuelta la página

Gustavo Gac-Artigas - Chilean poet and writer. Winner of the Poetry Park Award, Róterdam 1989, his poetry has been included in: *Multilingual Anthology: The Americas Poetry Festival of New York* (2019, 2021), *Multicultural Echoes* (CSU-Chico), *Enclave* (CUNY), *Cronopio, Letralia, Fonoteca de Poesía, Revista Kametsa, Todoliteratura,* and *The Nueva York Poetry Review*, etc. He is a member of the North American Academy of the Spanish Language (ANLE).

Canción de cuna

por Miguel Carpio

Me gusta dormir
en ríos amarillos y amargos,
      con canciones de cuna
      que me consuman por dentro
y me cierren los ojos
abriéndome la garganta
      a gritos.

Me gusta el arrullo
del fuego en mis vísceras,
      el un-dos, un-dos
      de la arcada profunda.

Me gusta que las ovejas que cuento
se tropiecen al andar
      al tratar de brincar la cerca de botellas
      donde apoyo la cabeza.

Me gusta esa canción
porque siempre que la escucho
sé que sólo queda descansar
y esperar que sea el final.

Miguel Carpio (1993). Ganó el premio Pablo Neruda con el poemario *Jazzologías* (2015). Fue seleccionado por la Unión Europea en la antología *Bolivia sub-35: Narrativas emergentes* por su libro de cuentos *Dos botellas más cerca de la muerte* (2021). Publicó textos en las revistas *Letralia*, *Marabunta*, *Cuaderno* y *88 Grados*.

Cuatro amores

por Itzel Torres

Corazones partidos,
el sonido de los sueños,
pasos marchitos,
almas desorientadas.

Recuerdos de cuatro amores,
los pocos que yo tuve,
uno amante de las flores,
los otros víctimas de pasiones.

«Yo» la ciega que lloró.
Cupido no me flechó.
La loca que gritó,
la que la diversión mató.

Último de todos,
quedado en el corazón,
ese que ya vivía,
quizá al que más amó.

Sólo el invierno eterno,
 sólo las primaveras secas,
sólo el verano floreado,
sólo testigos de la verdad fueron.

–¡Queredme! –susurra el dolor.
–No me temas –suplica alegre–. Tú y yo somos amigas,
sólo nosotras viviremos.

Abrazando el fuego,
lanzándose al hielo,
el dolor quemó el anhelo
y la soledad tomó el sosiego.

Itzel Torres (2006). Escritora y poetisa mexicana. Ha publicado en la revista digital "Cósmica Fanzine": "Atrapado en el tiempo" (entrada agosto) y "La última mirada" (entrada noviembre). También se encuentran sus poemas: "Mariposa muerta" (Antología "Renacer en primavera", Amazon) y "Hombre de cambio" (campaña "Alas de Mariposa").

Hoy no presto la felicidad

por Alexis Morales Valdera

a Yamil Díaz Gómez

¿Fui a la guerra? No recuerdo…
Quedé sentado en el puente
escribiendo una carta de desamor
prestando la felicidad.
He vuelto para entregarla
en el buzón del jardín.
Soy poeta de ese jardín perdido
poeta del dolor
poeta de las espinas poeta del poeta.
¿Regresé de la guerra? No recuerdo…
Fui un soldado desconocido
el flautista en la cruz
el hacedor de letras y de lluvia
el verdadero duque de Marlborough.
Después del huracán se ahogó mi guerra
repartí girasoles y fotos
y me entregué a los dioses verdaderos.
Es mejor ser fotógrafo en postguerra y besar el agua
y amar el puente roto donde se sienta mi hija.
Hoy no presto la felicidad
la guerra queda lejos.

Alexis Morales Valdera - Médico, nace en 1971(Cuba). Fue guionista de programas radiales . Publica en la revista Brotes. Durante años es miembro del taller los Kakafuacos dirigido por el escritor Yamil Díaz de la casa de cultura provincial. Obtiene mención en concurso de poesía municipal en Santa Clara. Ha publicado en revistas en España y EUA. Publica el poemario Pase de Visita con la editorial Z centuria en Argentina.

Cascabel

por Masiel M. Corona Santos

Entre ramas,
cuerpos abiertos se balancean,
duermen bajo aguas poco profundas.
Cabezas se elevan,
sudan conocimiento.
El aliento escapa de sus ojos.
   Oraciones,
sangre en un collar de hojas,
bocas poseídas sahúman lenguas.
Beber saliva de los animales corona la fuerza.
Laurel debajo de la almohada,
    agita los sueños.
Colócalas en tu ventana,
y en tu mano izquierda,
escribe deseos en ellas,
    quémalas.
El cuchillo en tu mano,
ahuyenta los espíritus,
   cae
      punta
        adentro.
Cambia tu rostro,
transita lo desconocido,
viaja sobre tu espalda
donde el sonido se alarga.
Recupera tu fuerza,
   eres ágil,
escalas como la hierba.
El humo produce visiones,
   purifica,
     protege,
      renueva.

Masiel M. Corona Santos es poeta bilingüe y líder comunitaria. M.A. Letras Hispánicas y Lingüística. Autora de *Cantos Revolucionarios*. Su trabajo aparece en revistas digitales, impresas, y antologías. Es fundadora de *Revista Raíces*, coeditora de *Revista Quimera* (Costa Rica). Colabora con Los Ángeles Poet Society y Centro Cultural de México.

la casa me recuerda siempre que mis manos están vacías

por Javier Fuentes Vargas

y si no es un corazón lo que aspiran a sostener,
que se acomoden en alguno de los espacios grises
donde pueden llorar tranquilamente toda la ausencia que soportan.
Mis manos son cada vez más viejas y se cansan hasta de colgar,
mi abuela besaba sus manos cada vez que la carne le fallaba,
nunca entendí el agradecimiento detrás de la traición.
Yo deseo de la carne que no entienda las señales del tiempo,
que, al oír su voz, no corra a soportar
todos los años que quieran colocar sobre ella.
Yo deseo de mis manos que, aunque no puedan sostener un corazón,
encuentren en la casa algo que no sea gris
y pueda decirme desde la frontera de los otros colores
el azul que adorna el cielo afuera de mi casa.

Yo deseo de la casa todo lo que pueda entregarme.

Javier Fuentes Vargas (Santa Ana, El Salvador, 2000). Poeta. Obra publicada: *La muerte llegará* (Artesanos & Editores, El Salvador, 2019), *Un lugar donde espero no morir sin conocer el odio* (Incendio Plaquettes, Guatemala, 2021) y *Vaho/Mist* (FlowerSong Press, Estados Unidos, 2021). Ha sido traducidos al inglés, esloveno y rumano.

Orden vital

por Rolando Reyes López

Primero una chispa, luego el tributo,
más tarde el recuerdo.

Pude besar las notas de esa canción,
sus trazos indefensos, su dolor más querido;
de mi flor emergió un grito, lo puse junto al almendro
y me fui a soñar sobre mi cama vacía.

Rolando Reyes López (Pedro Betancourt. Matanzas. 1969). Reside desde el año 1971 en el Municipio de Jovellanos. Matanzas. Cuba Graduado de Bachiller. Actualmente es jubilado por Baja Visión. Numerosos relatos breves y poemas suyos han sido publicados en revistas y antologías de varios países de Europa y Latinoamérica.

Nomatca Nehuatl
I Myself

por Odilia Galván Rodríguez

*Por los Poemas del maestro Francisco X. Alarcón S
nake Poems an Aztec Invocation*

yo misma
yo de los siete mares
hija de Yemayá
quien baila bien
las olas de dar y recibir
quien ha conocido la sal
de mil millones de lágrimas
que ha pagado mis deudas
durante todos estos años
yo que respeto toda la vida

yo mujer de la tierra
yo rosa con espinas
yo corazón de tuna
yo lengua afilada
yo buscadora de la verdad
yo encantadora de serpientes
yo machetera por la justicia
yo amante del amor
yo aspirante a visionario
y veraz
yo virgen-puta
yo mujer que resiste
no más de lo que puedo
yo mujer sabia
yo herbolaria urbano-
descendiente de curanderas
yo escritora
un altavoz
profesora

yo sembradora de semillas
nomatca nehuatl

Odilia Galván Rodríguez, poet, writer, editor-publisher, and activist, is the author of six volumes of poetry. Her latest book from FlowerSong Press is *The Color of Light ~ Poems to the Mexica and Orisha Energies*. She is also a co-editor, along with the late Francisco X. Alarcón, of the award-winning anthology *Poetry of Resistance: Voices for Social Justice*, The University of Arizona Press. She is the editor-in-chief and publisher at Prickly Pear Publishing & Nopalli Press. Additionally, she has worked as the editor for several magazines, including Tricontinental Magazine in Havana, Cuba, Switchgrass Review, Corpus Christi, and online – Cloud Women's Quarterly Journal and Anacua Literary Arts Journal.

Armazón de claves

por Nelson Roque Pereira

Duele tanto partir al renglón sin un abrazo, al esqueleto que abriga la nostalgia; muchos días el hombre ha despertado en el centro de un suicidio con rabia de un proyecto venturoso.

Pienso que tendré piel de otoño para toda la vida, no he podido con la máscara de isla, y no sé si confesar lo que me susurran los versos amarillos hundiéndose en la carne.

Muchos días, encuentro el jardín sin sueños; le zarandeo al revés, para que caigan lápidas y cuadrantes, el grito de nuevas ramas en la siembra del mundo.

De mi cama cuelgan los cuadros que atrapé en la adolescencia: un parque con pinos borrosos, la vieja estatua de la madre con su hijo, frutas que empinan el pecho desde el mito de la soledad, roedores de páginas fuera de su tiempo y siempre la misma voz desde el interior, como un libro de cabecera apresurando al hombre a tomar las calles bajo los ojos de la diez de la mañana.

Si he permitido a Dios fuera del cielo, es que busco a otros que agiten versos bajo la lluvia de sal que desencadenan los días.

Si alguien me dijese de otros puertos, aire o espuma, remaría al otro río, contra el curso hambriento que desovan los barrancos por los que despeño.

Cómo no amar el cuerpo donde bebió Borges, dolores que destejen causa y efecto, viviendo sobre olas, tan cerca y distante, en inquietos segadores que revientan la vaina del poema contra sus vientres, sin haber saciado toda el hambre del verso.

Nelson Roque Pereira - Pertenece a POETAP y ELILUC; obra publicada "Por los cauces de la noche"; "Libro Internacional Puente de palabras XIII 2016"; en Antología mundial "Poetas siglo veintiuno"; "El abrazo del Nogal de Daimuz", antología Lorquiana tomo II; "Ágora de la poesía"; "Alhucema" Revista Internacional de Teatro y Literatura; en varias antologías.

Viento

por Jorge Millán

A veces le hablo al viento
con mi voz ronca y agónica,
con mi boca torcida y deforme,
con mi lengua seca y lacerada.
Le hablo y le digo lo que siento.

A veces le hablo al viento,
con los ojos cerrados
desde mi soledad desolada,
desde mi tristeza infundada,
y abro los párpados de nuevo
para recordar que no estoy ciego.

A veces le hablo al viento
porque siento que es el único que entiende,
porque me convenzo que sólo él me escucha,
esperando que su respuesta no se reduzca
sólo a una perorata displicente.

A veces le hablo al viento
deseando que mis palabras no sólo se las lleve
sino que las regrese con un dejo de esperanza,
mientras vislumbro en la nocturna lontananza
las estrellas brillantes como copos de nieve.

Jorge Millán Nieto es egresado de la Licenciatura en Lengua y Literatura Hispánicas de la Universidad Veracruzana. Ha publicado los textos *Fantasma sin límites*, *Desdoblamiento onírico* (cuento), *El minimalismo como arte narrativo…* y *Los pueblos indígenas como modelo de identidad cultural* (ensayo) en las revistas Nudo Gordiano, Monociclo, Espora y Funk, respectivamente. Asimismo, es uno de los autores participantes en la antología literaria "Mar de Tinta", próxima a ser publicada por la editorial homónima independiente junto con otros escritores de México y Latinoamérica.

Otras

por Edna Ochoa

Callada penumbra de tus años doce
cuando el ojo de Dios muerto a brochazos
no vigilaría nunca más desde el altar de la Virgen.
Ni los sermones del clérigo
ascenderían por los cabellos hasta susurrar extrañas culpas.

La casa y el colegio revelaron nuevo rostro.
Uniforme blanco
que ciñó el volantín que alzaba tu cuerpo y tierra confundidos.

Un camellón de palmeras.　　　　　Aldabones de las casas.
Aquella fila larga de niñas detenidas en el papel
cuando el flash cegó un instante.

En la pared mensajes.　　　　　Un trozo de Biblia

Darío en la mesa con «Versos de otoño»
y del tragaluz la sombra del gato proyectándose
sobre la jarra de agua y el mantel tan largo
cuando supiste que los años crecían…
Que la noche bebería tu rostro
como vaso de residuos de estrellas.

Edna Ochoa is the author of many books, including *Fugaces/ Flashes*, *Jirones de ayer*, *Sombra para espejos*, and *La cerca circular*, among others. She is translator to Spanish of Zoot Suit by Luis Valdez, The Frog and His Friends Save Humanity by Víctor Villaseñor, and *The Magic of Mariachi* by Steven P. Schneider. Ochoa is professor at The University of Texas Rio Grande Valley.

Retrato poético: Aliona

por Juan Manuel Díaz

Durante el ocaso entre los Urales
sobre estepas perdidas
nace una niña de cabellos de rojizo oro

Es la hija del Sol
con mirada flamígera
incendia ciudades de mármol y acero

Humanos ciegos por su luz
intentan tocar la piel blanca
hecha de estrellas

Es una musa
cuyas huellas son cenizas
su tacto calienta e incendia memorias

En sánscrito la oración escrita
No te vayas
el fuego incendia y ama
abrasa y abraza
su tacto calienta e incendia memorias

Ella es fuego
fuego animal
fuego devorador
siempre fuego

Elegida por dioses y mortales
es la de Troya
también la de Moscú

Primera Roma

Tercera Roma
Eterna Roma
es el faro en la Torre Roja

Juan Manuel Díaz nació el 11 de octubre de 1985 en la Ciudad de México. Escritor cuya obra está integrada por cuento, novela, poesía y microficción. Escribe para el periódico La Izquierda Diario, y las revistas Ideas de Izquierda y Penumbria sobre cine, arte y literatura. Su obra se ha publicado en revistas como Tlacuache, Penumbria, Zorro Lector, Anapoyesis y Morbífica.

Realidad casi poética

por Claudia Excaret Santos Campusano

El entierro
La institución
Los uniformados

La familia,
la institución,
los uniformados
y el último pase de lista.

Su nombre,

la espera

la

espera

(la espera de que el silencio nos aplastara,
la espera de que el silencio nos derrumbara,
la espera de que el silencio nos enfrentara

a la realidad)

Su ausencia

La espera

El uniformado grito de «presente».

Su nombre

El ahora acompañado
pero dubitativo grito de «presente»

Su nombre
y
la firme respuesta conjunta del «presente».

Claudia Excaret Santos Campusano (she/her) is a Mexican poet, interpreter, and content creator. She usually focuses on the writing of academic essays. Her poetry has been published in the Canadian digital magazine *Fleas on the Dog*.

«Aquí...»

por Eduardo Villarreal de los Reyes

I
Salieron al viento,
dejando la casa paterna,
el huerto, el postigo,
la voz antigua de la abuela
que cada domingo
recordaba capítulos de su vida.
Se fueron a aprender otra canción,
otro lenguaje y tener otra ilusión.

Un muro, un desierto, un río.
Laberinto y dragón
en un juego de vida, muerte u olvido.

II
Me prometiste la corona de la felicidad,
la multiplicación de panes y pescados,
pero no me hablaste
de las llagas de mis manos
ni las espinas en mi frente.

No hubo Moisés para separar las aguas del río
ni viento de oriente para secarlo.
Solamente el desierto de la tentación y la queja.

No hubo necesidad de las nueve plagas,
fue suficiente el vaho de la bestia del desierto.

Tampoco hubo lluvia de panes sin levadura
pero de la nada surgió el milagro.

III
Aquí el césped no crece
o solo y mágicamente se corta de un día a otro.
Aquí las casas se van construyendo solas,
cada clavo con su madera y de ladrillo a ladrillo
de igual manera.
Aquí las casas se limpian solas por voluntad propia

o nunca se ensucian, al igual que la ropa.
Aquí la comida se cocina sola a diario y
se multiplica el arroz, los tamales,
el pan dulce y las tortillas.
Aquí los automóviles se auto limpian.
La fruta y la verdura
—sin importar el sol olvidado—
llegan al mercado por una suerte de milagro
sin rastro de sudor y manos.
Son los invisibles,
los que solamente son vistos si cruzan el río.
Aprendices de muertos buscando un milagro.
Aquí nadie muere ahogado en el río.
Aquí no me refleja ningún espejo
y no cuento para ningún censo.
No vamos, no volvemos, no existimos.
Somos bocas guardando un secreto.
Aquí las manos no descansan
ni habrá tumba ni cementerio
para los que vivieron de incógnitos.

Van buscando algo que un día fue nuestro,
buscando otro signo que nos diga,
que estamos de regreso a Aztlán.

Eduardo Villarreal de los Reyes (H. Matamoros, Tamaulipas). Su obra se incluye en *Poetas de Ayer y Hoy en Tamaulipas* (1983), compilado por Ramón Durón Ruiz. En 1983 obtuvo primer lugar en Cuento y Poesía en la Facultad de Ciencias de la Comunicación (UANL). En 1996 el Festival Internacional de Otoño le otorgó el Reconocimiento a las Expresiones del Arte. En 1985 es candidato al Premio Nacional de la Juventud CREA por el estado de Nuevo León en el renglón de Creación Literaria. Ha participado en diversos encuentros de escritores y su obra se encuentra en varias antologías y periódicos. Es director fundador del Foro Cultural «Poesía en Atril» (2016 al presente), que presenta lecturas mensuales de cuento y poesía de escritores del noreste de México y Texas. Publicó en 2019 su libro *Ahora pregunto yo*. Es director de la Casa del Poeta «Pablo Neruda» en la ciudad de Brownsville, Texas, fundada en noviembre de 2019 siendo la primera fuera de México perteneciente a la Asociación Civil Casa del Poeta. También en 2019 recibió un reconocimiento de la Sociedad de Geografía y Estadística del Estado de México, la Academia de Literatura y Poesía de la SOMEGEM y las Casas del Poeta A.C. En 2020 publica *A veces la poesía* y *Todo de Nuevo*. En 2021 es recopilador de la antología *Lustro*, libro con que se celebró los cinco años de Poesía en Atril.

Después de Noé

por Citlalli H. Xochitiotzin

El dolor es una mancha en el ojo
lágrima diminuta extinta entre la respiración y un beso
entre el duermevela y el día endurecido de volutas y polen
aquí donde los árboles suelen caminar
con su viento de hojarasca seca
y un sueño aterido, donde los metales del viento
no causan más dolor que el necesario
como caminar sobre fuego, como dolerse de
estaquitas en el pecho
y morir de a poquito, lento, así de pequeño
para decir adiós y no mover los labios
ni el brillo de la pupila dolerse así de pellizquitos.
Para no morir completamente
he de iluminar la casa, el parque, la habitación
de esta inmensidad, pesa sobre la extinta
palabra nunca pronunciada
así de estúpida es
la explanada de esta avenida llamada
Diálogo.
Y un silencio de orgullo dureza, torpeza
es el tráfico,
corazones de gato, así de arañitos
de asonancias en el alma de los enamorados
corren peligro por el beso, el tacto de la mano,
el contacto con los dedos, el brillo de los ojos.
Un día en la avenida estuvimos desnudos de canciones
y no supimos cantar la misma melodía,
un mundo prohíbe tocarnos
y nos encarcela en un cubrebocas,
cientos de razones en papeles y códigos de
un corto mirar en autobuses,
nadie gritará: ¡se muere el torpe!
Se escalda la frase, se esconde la vida,
Tanta muerte acostumbra los reflectores más suntuosos,
cómo, si nos sigue el dolor de docenas de muertes

Y el pudor, comprometido con todo
y nada, él lo mismo, nada,
no somos atrevidos besadores de enfermos,
el loco tiene su fe muy bien cardada en el listón,
y la prudencia del drama se llama estupidez de
obtener el dolor de a traguitos
hasta que se muera la sombra y Noé nos llame nuevamente
al arca transformados en Ave Fénix.
La odisea mayor, es amar, con la piel puesta
en el alma, y mirándonos como Dios:
sin atravesar el zoológico.
sin regresar al diluvio llorosos…
Dios, perdona al torpe, olvida el arcoíris, su arcoíris.

Citlalli H. Xochitiotzin. Mexicana. Nació en 1957. Perteneciente a la generación de escritores de los 50. Estudió Sociología en la Universidad Autónoma de México y Filosofía UAT. Poeta, ensayista, escritora, filosofía. Incluida en antologías de México y de otros países. Tiene libros de poesía, historia y ensayo, entre los que destacan: *Geometría de la incertidumbre* (CONACULTA-Universidad de Monterrey), *Días del polvo* (UNAM. *Memorial de la sangre* (UNAM), *Fulgor de alimentos* (Ed. Errante Editor), *Poemas sobre los techos* (Ed. Letras de Barro), *Historia del edificio del Tribunal de Justicia* (Ed. TSJ), la traducción del *Libro de guía arquitectónica de Tlaxcala* al inglés y la biografía del maestro Xochitiotzin, en tres tomos, etc. Paralelamente a su labor literaria trabaja en la organización, fomento y difusión de la cultura en México y los EE. UU. Es fundadora de instituciones (fundó 44 bibliotecas) y participa en los movimientos sociales de las garantías individuales, la paz y la mujer, desde los años 70. Actualmente es presidenta de la Fundación Desiderio Hernández Xochitiotzin, presidenta del Seminario de Cultura Mexicana, editora de Cuarto Creciente y coordinadora del colectivo Malitzin. Ha obtenido premios en España y México en reconocimiento a su trabajo como poeta. Su obra ha sido traducida al inglés y al ruso.

Nubes condescendientes
por Mario R. Montani

Son castillos de lluvia y de nieve
que en lo inmenso del cielo circulan,
arrastrados por brisas muy leves
y también por los vientos que aúllan.

Sus torres con negras almenas
do ecos retumban sin fin
semejan columnas eternas
que al rayo contemplan surgir.

De tal figura en lo alto
se divisan los pendones,
ora teñidos de blanco,
ora de grises colores.

Y el relámpago baja
en su carro de fuego
con invisibles alas
que anticipan el trueno.

Cubrirán las nubes
la luz de la tarde,
allá donde mueren
los sonidos graves.

Y poco a poco,
como si nada,
caerán las gotas
en la calzada.

Y la lluvia
en su afán,
mojará
la ciudad.

Nubes,
agua,
cae
ya…

**

Mario R. Montani vive en Bahía Blanca, Argentina. Ha estudiado Letras en la Universidad Nacional del Sur. Su colección de relatos *El Castillo Gris y otros cuentos* fue publicada en 2009 por Editorial Dunken.

Domingos con sol

por Carlos Álvarez Pazos

¡Domingos con sol!
¡Soles domingueros!

En el salmo azul del cielo
reverbera un sol radiante
invitando a las tempraneras horas
a volar en mil cometas
y a volverse al alma una cometa,
al corazón un cóndor que flamea
la majestuosa danza de sus alas
e inflama de horizontes los caminos.

El joven riachuelo
golpetea con latidos cristal de agua
las iridiscentes piedras de la orilla.

¡Domingos con sol!
¡A madrugar y arrebatar al día
sus racimos de alborozo!
Los mercados se vuelven enjambre de murmullos,
vendimia de aromas y de frutales colores.

El sanjuanito multicolor de las polleras
alegra las laderas y caminos
de los caseríos y los pueblos de los Andes.
Los campanarios lanzan en revuelo
repiques de oro y azules mariposas
convocando a la misa de las doce.

La juerga de los niños
resuena en el laberinto del encanto.
Los enamorados arrebólanse en besos
y un torbellino de anémonas
estremece en fugaz voracidad
la enredadera de sus cuerpos.

¡Domingos de solsticio de verano,
esplendidez de soles domingueros,
himno de la alegría
del bullir de los instantes de la Vida
que vibra, se extingue y nunca vuelve!

Carlos Álvarez **Pazos** (Cuenca, Ecuador, 1944-) fue docente e investigador de la Universidad de Cuenca, donde se especializó en Lengua y Literatura. Obtiene titulaciones en el Instituto Caro y Cuervo (Bogotá, Colombia) y en el Centro de Estudios Regionales Andinos «Bartolomé de las Casas» (Cusco, Perú). Es autor de siete libros sobre lexicografía kichwa-castellana y cultura andina, cinco como autor único y dos en coautoría. Además, es miembro de la Casa de Cultura Ecuatoriana (Núcleo del Azuay). Se ha presentado en varios países como expositor y ponente en cursos, simposios, talleres de capacitación y otros eventos sobre lengua y cultura andinas. El poema antologado en este libro forma parte de la obra *Y la vida sigue crepitando: poemas del pasado y del presente,* que se editará próximamente.

El hondazo

por Luis Jorge Verano

¡La piedra!
¡La piedra partida me perforó la frente!
Y era tu beso, niño,
que cabalgó las calle en hormigas
esperando ver elefantes
sentados en las plazas
y sólo encontró palomas ingenuas,
        amando vuestras casas.

A la quebrada de la tarde
hundiendo la sangre del último trino
        en el espacio.

¡Honda,
llegaste enhorquetada en el tiempo
cuando la realidad del elefante
se desvaneció en la plaza.
La dejaron tirada en la orilla de tu alma,
descuidada,
seres de otras galaxias
después de la glaciación de la tierra
(la usaban para extinguir las mariposas
temerosos que estas interfirieran
en la actividad extraterrestre).

A la quebrada de la tarde
hundiendo la sangre del último trino
        en el espacio.

Nota: A todo niño HUMANO se solicita amar el cielo poblado de alas. Es muy triste tener un cielo raso y pájaros de cartulina que no aman ni trinan. Sinceramente agradecido, Otro Humano.

Luis Jorge Verano es un escritor y poeta argentino, radicado en la cuidad de Roldán. Obtuvo reconocimientos locales y mención de honor en el Concurso Internacional de Poesía «El IV Quijote de Plata». Ha dictado conferencias y fue miembro integrante de la asociación cultural de Rosario Grupo Rosarino Caracol (de poetas) entre otros. Publicó en diferentes diarios y revistas de su país. Obra publicada: *Semillas esparcidas* (1982), *Para el capitán celeste* (1987), *El compendio de la lechuza* (2007), *Cirylo Pané, una memoria viva* (2011) y *Motivos de la fuente* (2018). Apasionado del universo de las letras y la lectura, en la actualidad publica su nuevo material en la página de Facebook «Hebras» y trabaja una novela.

BOUNDLESS - YOUTH
POEMS & ART

SELECTED & EDITED
BY EDWARD VIDAURRE

Christian Hilario, 6 years old

Hace dos meses murió mi perro

por Mía Hernández

la mascota que era parte de mi familia
que nos acompañó por más de 6 años
sin ti queda vacía la casa
extraño mucho tus caricias y compañía
extrañando tus travesuras
pero lo que extraño más
es llegar a casa y saber que ya nadie me recibe

Cuando suena el timbre, nadie ladra
extraño el espacio donde dormías
un espacio, vacío
tu piel era suave y de color blanco
fuiste mi mejor amigo: cariñoso, juguetón,
chistoso y amable
yo sé que no te has ido
sé que estás en un lugar mucho mejor
algún día espero volver a encontrarme
con una mascota como tu

Mía Hernández was born on February 22, 2005 and is a junior in La Joya isd Early College. She used to play violin; it was her passion; she has stopped playing it but hopes to continue in the future. She is the middle child out of 3 children.

"Mirrored" by Asya Mia Hinojosa, 15 years old

His love for music is never ending

by Gina Medina

His love for music is neverending.
Do you think you could relate?
The way he does?
The way we do?
Do you think his shoulder is healed up well enough?
Enough to love more than he should?
Enough to feel more than he would?
Do you think you could relate?
The way he does?
The way we do?
In the end, he became his own story.
Do you think you could create yours?
Is it enough to make you warm?
Enough to relate to it like he does?
The way we all do?

Gina Medina is a 9th grader and is currently attending La Joya Early College High School. Gina ,in her free time, likes to play instruments. She likes to write about how she views others or things from a different perspective.

Por la noche

por Alicia D. Gómez

Todo está oscuro y silencioso.
puedes escuchar todos los pensamientos
en tu mente debido al silencio.
no hay movimiento a la vista.
todos están dormidos y, sin embargo,
aquí estoy con un millón de pensamientos corriendo por mi cabeza.
las estrellas brillan intensamente
y también la luna.

Mirar el cielo nocturno me deshace
de cualquier pensamiento en mi mente
y me libera de cualquier estrés.
encuentro la paz.
por la noche, me quedo despierta
para admirar la belleza de la luna y las estrellas.
disfruto viendo la luna por la noche.
alivia mi mente
y se deshace de cualquier pensamiento.

Puedes respirar el aire fresco
cuando estás afuera admirando la noche.
respiro y libero cualquier tensión de mis hombros.
me trae paz.
por la noche, pienso y pienso.
por la noche, me quedo despierta y admiro su belleza.
el silencio, la luna y las estrellas.
en ese momento
estoy libre de cualquier pensamiento
y solo disfruto de la tranquilidad que trae la noche.

Alicia is a 11th grader and is currently attending La Joya Early College High School. Alicia enjoys painting or reading a good book in her free time. She is a determined and independent person and enjoys helping others.

My best friend
by Jenni Zamorano

The one who's always there for me
The one who never leaves my side
She looks at me with her beautiful ocean eyes
Making my day a million times better
Her smile can warm anyone's heart

My pretty girl
Her name: Nova
Like the star
Suits her well as
She can light up the night
Even on my worst days i know
I can count on her to make me feel better
As she is
My best friend

Jenni is a 10th grader and is currently attending La Joya Early College High School. Jenni Zamorano in her free time likes to spend time with her friends and family, especially her dog. She likes to write about pretty much anything.

Sister

by Janeysi Villarreal

She feels lost and unworthy
She struggled at such a young age,
Not feeling or seeing the love her siblings show her,
Feeling every moment she spends alive is worthless.

She feels scared and confused
That she sees and hears things that we do not,
Her mind wanders to the darkest part
And she watches her true fears come to life.

She feels betrayed by the people she loves
The way they take her to someone to talk to
Her feelings needing a pill or two
That she seems better without.

She feels isolated and forgotten
They watch her every move,
For when she makes one mistake
And she's gone again.

She feels tired of living
The way she feels her life is completely controlled
As her family does nothing about it,
And she now feels her medication is now useful

She feels scared, guilty, and regret
But it was too late
Her body gets ruined
And she needs to start over again.

Janeysi Marie Villarreal is a 17-year-old 12th grader and is currently attending La Joya Early College High School. Janeysi in her free time likes to spend time with her family. She likes to write letters to her family members and friends to make them feel special and loved.

Hermana

por Janeysi Villarreal

Ella se siente perdida e indigna
Ella luchó a una edad tan joven,
Sin sentir ni ver el amor que le muestran sus hermanas,
Sentir que cada momento que pasa aquí es inútil.

Ella se siente asustada y confundida
Que ella ve y oye cosas que nosotros no,
Su mente vaga a la parte más oscura
Y observa cómo sus verdaderos miedos cobran vida.

Ella se siente traicionada por las personas que ama.
La forma en que la llevan con alguien con quien hablar
Sus sentimientos necesitan una pastilla o dos
Que ella parece mejor sin ellas.

Ella se siente aislada y olvidada
Ellos miran cada movimiento de ella
Para cuando comete un error
Y se ha ido de nuevo.

Ella se siente cansada de vivir
La forma en que siente que su vida está completamente controlada.
Como su familia no hace nada para ayudarla,
Y ahora siente que su medicación es útil

Ella se siente asustada, culpable y arrepentida
Pero fue demasiado tarde
Su cuerpo se arruina
Y ella necesita empezar de nuevo.

Janeysi Marie Villarreal is a 17-year-old 12th grader and is currently attending La Joya Early College High School. Janeysi in her free time likes to spend time with her family. She likes to write letters to her family members and friends to make them feel special and loved.

Loneliness

by Audrey Moreno

There is always a reason why I love myself
or something that is not going well

There is nothing that I feel in my heart
everything is shattered

Like a dream has come to an end
I have lost the way of seeing

I hate being alone
with my thoughts, and feelings

Being alone is painful
it makes my heart sing

Loneliness is like the wind
sometimes it can be soft, sometimes strong

I wish there was
someone who would come talk to me

About all of my friends
but there is no one

That would like to talk to me
I feel alone

The girl who had many friends
the one that everyone wanted to be

The girl who
maybe one day

Could go back
to not being alone

Audrey Moreno is a 10th grader and is currently attending La Joya ECHS.Audrey likes to dance, and spend time with her friends and family. She likes to write about her life,and how people around has motivated her to shape her into the young woman she is today.

A Symphony
by Nayleen Arredondo

Music is a marvelous form of art
My favorite kind of music is classical music
It soothes my soul, like a leaf gliding through the wind
My favorite instruments are the piano and violin
By themselves they are amazing

When played together it's like a symphony from heaven.

They both just connect perfectly together
When you close your eyes

The music takes you to a
magical place where all your worries disappear

As if the music washes it away
There are so many types of music
All with different meanings to them

When you hear a song that you like for the first time
It's like at that moment you made a connection
For some people, the connection is strong
It's like a symphony

that has been missing in their hearts for a long time...

Nayleen Arredondo is a 12 grader and is currently attending La Joya ECHS. Nayleen in her free time likes to play video games and help her parents. Nayleen likes to write about experiences she has had in her lifetime that has changed her into who she is as a person.

Ella lloraba

by Ashley Castillo

Y no entendía
Por qué su corazón
Se partía
Sentía que
Todo su mundo
Lo perdía
Desesperada
En medio de su agonía
Cuando sentía que moría
Llegó una luz
Que la llenó de alegría
Abrió los ojos
Vio a su alrededor
Todo tiene color
Había pasado
Lo peor
Sonrió cuando
Entendió
Que nada estaba mal
Nada había sido real
Todo en su mente pasó

She cried and cried

por Ashley Castillo

And didn't understand
Why her heart
was so broken
She felt
Like the world
was fading away
Desperate
In the midst of her agony
When she felt like dying
There was a light
That filled her with happiness
She opened her eyes
and saw around her
Everything has color
The worst
has already passed
She smiled
when she understood
That nothing was bad
Nothing had been real
Everything was all in her head

Ashley Castillo is a 15 year old sophomore that is attending her second year at La Joya Early College High School.

Growing up
by Aylín Hernández

Being a kid is hard
Growing up is harder
As kids we wait impatiently,
with shaking hands and heads full of hope
For the days in which we can stand all on our own

Growing up is very difficult
It means having to mature as you grow older
If you don't mature as you grow
You will have the stress of everyone judging you

As kids grow
Adults tend to pressure them
They expect us to do things the way they want

Even though being a young adult is great
It is not the same as being a kid
There is no shame in wanting to find happiness again
And not wanting anything to change

Aylín Hernández is currently a sophomore in high school at La Joya Early College and will graduate in 2024 with her associates degree. This is her second time writing and publishing a poem. Aylín in her free time likes to read and write about her past life experiences.

Crecer
por Aylín Hernández

Ser un niño es difícil
Crecer es más difícil
De niños esperamos con impaciencia
con manos temblorosas y cabezas llenas de esperanza
Por los días en los que podemos estar solos

Crecer es muy difícil
Significa tener que madurar con el tiempo
Si no maduras a medida que creces
Tendrás el estrés de que todos te juzguen

Cuando los niños crecen,
Los adultos tienden a presionarlos
Esperan que hagamos las cosas como ellos quieren

Aunque ser un adulto joven es genial
No es lo mismo que ser niño
No hay vergüenza en querer volver a encontrar la felicidad
Y no querer que nada cambie

Aylín Hernández is currently a sophomore in high school at La Joya Early College and will graduate in 2024 with her associates degree. This is her second time writing and publishing a poem. Aylín in her free time likes to read and write about her past life experiences.

Lo que vi

por Kaylee A. Perales

Mis ojos no me engañan,
Sé lo que vi.
Esos sentimientos se han quedado conmigo.
La sensación de hormigueo arrastrándose por toda mi piel
Es como sentir las cuchillas atravesándome.
Sé que vi ese coche moverse, Eso no es mentira.

Mi mente no está jugando malas pasadas,
Está ahí pero borroso.
Las emociones siguen aquí,
Pero están más domesticadas ahora.
Se movían tantas botellas
Y se siguieron agregando más.

Los recuerdos están desapareciendo,
Aunque no quiero recordar,
Pero el sentimiento sigue ahí.
Todo es un gran desastre
Pero el panorama general aún permanece.

Todo es tan diferente
Trato de elegir todas las piezas de este rompecabezas
Pero parece que no puedo encontrarlas todas.
La respuesta no está clara.

Nada encaja y las piezas no parecen cuadrar
Pero no puedes mirarme y decir que todo está bien.
No digas que las cosas no han cambiado
Porque si eso fuera cierto no habría este lío.
Si eso fuera cierto, ese coche no se habría movido
Esas botellas no habrían seguido sumando.
Mi mente no estaría en este cansado lugar.

Kaylee A. Perales is a 12th grader and is currently attending La Joya Early College High School. Kaylee A. Perales in her free time likes to listen to music and spend time with her dog. She likes to write about her personal life and her mind and thoughts.

Decepción con felicidad

por Nadiea Cantú-Hernández

5'6 mide la chica de pelo rubio
la que se ha enamorado

De los ojos cafés del chico que aún la mira como princesa
después de los momentos desafortunados
Y la decepción de su vida
Ella se esconde detrás de una pared
que ella ha construido alrededor
Él, de pelo negro

aún no se daba cuenta lo que le esperaba
detrás de la mujer que ella era
Siempre con una sonrisa detrás de la máscara

y los ojos brillantes
ella impresionaba a la gente
Menos ha él...

Él era el único que no la miraba por la sonrisa que fingía
Él simulaba no verla cuando él de hecho
siempre la admiraba
Mejores amigos se hicieron
Él a su lado y ella a lado de él
Inseparables puedes decir

Las mariposas que ella sentía cuando estaba con él

La sonrisa que él causaba
La seguridad que él le daba
Todo era el chico de ojos cafés y pelo negro

Pero no eran oficiales...
Debajo del sol brillante y el cielo azul
Con rosas rojas y el globo en su mano

Ella dijo que sí
El, de 5'11 se enamoró de ella
La chica de pelo rubio

Nadia Cantú-Hernández is a 11th grader and is currently attending La Joya Early College High School. Nadiea in her free time likes to work and she likes to write about her emotions and moments where she's felt happy, sometimes even sad.

Unspoken Words in a Field of Flowers

by Tem Ramírez

I can feel the wind blow past us as we watch
a large field of grass and flowers move and dance
to the rhythm of the earth.

I can feel your warmth.
I can sense your smile from where you sit
and it's the warmest I have felt in my entire life.

I've come too close to the sun and now I can feel
my skin disintegrating painfully
but the burn is so captivating.
It's addicting.

I come closer and feel the sun
burning and screaming in fiery delight

We both stare for a second and then start to laugh
the sun explodes and tears us apart.
now our pieces drift about and intertwine slowly in the
vacuum of space.

Like a tango, we dance until we
drift apart and hope to come across again
I can still feel the remnants of your heart embedded in mine In my memory, I
will always remember your supernova

Our world.
Our death and separation.

You snap at me and bring me back to the field
I missed you so much.
I hold you and feel your heartbeat.
Thank you, my love
I've missed your warmth

Tem is an 11th grader and is currently attending La Joya Early College. Tem in their free time likes to listen to music, bake and write about strong feelings and significant events in their lives as an outlet for their emotions. They are also published in Boundless 2020.

Gianelle Flores, 17 years-old

Something more than a game

by Shendel Lozano

Basketball

Dribble,

     run,

          walk,

               and shoot

Relieves my stress, &
makes me happy

Five people on the court to help
But I feel like all the pressure is on me

People in the stands are cheering me on
to some this sport is just a game
to me it is more
it is a lifestyle

There is no feeling like stealing the ball
Or shooting a three pointer
Five individuals working as one
Never giving up on each other no matter what

Shendel Lozano is a 12th grader and is currently attending La Joya Early College High School. Shendel Lozano in her free time likes to spend time with her family and friends. She likes to write about things that make her happy.

Overcoming
by Kristal Vivas

Fears

We all have fears

Some of us deal with many fears

That it feels like we're suffocating

While others don't have that many

Spiders, snakes, sharks

You can fear anything

Heights, oceans, enclosed spaces

I used to be fearful of many things

How I looked

How I talked

Of saying the wrong thing

Fears
It just made my life harder

Harder than it was supposed to be

I learned that although fears are hard to overcome

Trying to overcome them is better than not trying at all

Kristal Vivas is 16 years old and is currently in 11th grade at La Joya Early College High School. In her free time, she likes to spend time with her friends and family.

Things Change

by Melissa Ann Cantú

"This is America" my dad says smiling at the tv
He watched a singer in a luscious gold dress sing the National Anthem
The notes echoed against our tall ceiling, her stunning vibrato had me in a trance
He had tears in his eyes and with a proud smile
he says it again, but softer, sweeter:
"This is America mi'ja"

I smile softly, the look on my father's face
forever etched in my mind
I was no more than 8 years old
I'm 17 now and things are different
I'm different.

The way I see the world and this country has changed.
But that's the way of life isn't it?
Things change.

The way my dad looks at the tv when the national anthem plays has changed.
My mom's face when she turns on the news or opens her phone has changed.
It feels as though everything is changing.
Or maybe it's me changing?

Maybe none of this has changed at all,
just the way I view the world and my life has.
Things change, but what things?
Are we the ones who change while the world around us stays stagnant?

Or does the world change before our eyes while we remain the same?
I was 8 years old, now I'm 17
and things have changed.

Melissa Ann Cantú is a junior and is currently attending La Joya High School. Melissa likes to spend time with her dog and playing her instrument. She likes to write about fantasy, her faith, and life experiences.

Nos fallaste

por Debanhi I. Flores Cantú

Ha pasado un año,
Y sigo sin olvidar que nos fallaste.

Nos dejaste las cosas claras,
Pero nos hacías sentir culpable de todo.
Nos fallaste.

Pero dime, señor,
¿Cuál fue la razón?

Nos abandonaste,
Nos criticaste,
Te marchaste,
Y nos fallaste.

Pero dime, señor,
¿Qué debe hacer una niña sin su padre?

Eras frío,
Frío con tus palabras,
Frío con tus acciones,
Frío con tus propios hijos.
Y simplemente, nos fallaste.

Pero dime, señor,
¿Cuál fue la razón?
¿Qué debe hacer una niña sin su padre?

Debanhi is a senior at La Joya Early College High School. In her free time, she likes to hangout with her family and friends, as well as do extracurricular activities. Poetry tends to be her stress reliever because it describes her emotions through a couple of lines.

Felicidad

por Daniel Ramírez

Yo estoy feliz.
La forma en que mis amigos me traen
la felicidad es una bendición para mí.
Me da la felicidad al saber
que mis amigos están para mí,
y saben que yo también estoy.
Yo estoy feliz.

He tenido personas que me dejaron, lo cual me hizo
triste pero también feliz.
Estaba triste porque se habían ido.
Estaba feliz de que fueran parte de mi vida
y que aprendí algunas cosas sobre lo que
debería y no debería hacer.
Yo estoy feliz.

Estoy feliz de que todavía tengo mis
amigos y familiares conmigo.
Han traído tanta alegría en
mi vida que les sigo agradeciendo cada
momento que puedo.
También me han recordado cuán
agradecidos están también por tenerme.
Estoy lleno de felicidad.

Daniel Ramírez is a 11th grader and is currently attending La Joya Early College High School. Daniel Ramírez likes to play video games, workout, and read in his free time. He likes to write about experiences, lessons, and events that have happened before in his life and historical events.

The Pond of the World

by Jaziel De La Rosa

The man sat at the edge of the pond
vibrant fishes jumped out
the moon reflected brightly

lost in the eyes of the moon, he started to ponder
the man had been nothing but a failure

No love
No Greatness
No Success

everything they had told him he would achieve never arrived
It did not matter because he had a big decision coming up
this would finally prove he had courage

POP!

the moon was no longer reflecting in the pond
With the brightness of the moon no longer visible
the pond was visible
fishes swam around lost in a small pond wishing for freedom

Jaziel De la Rosa was born April 4, 2005 in McAllen, Texas. He is currently a Junior attending La Joya Early College High School. He enjoys reading and sports. His favorite thing to write about is the harsh realities of life.

Fouad Reda, age 9

Ansiedad

por María Magallón

Busco la salida
de este lugar tan tenebroso
busco las respuestas
de las preguntas que me cargo
¿Qué es lo que te pasa?
¿Por qué tanto temor?
¿Acaso eres cobarde?
¿O por qué tanto pavor?
estoy tan agotada
de no poder ni hablar
de no poder hacer nada
sin sentir esta ansiedad
no quiero ser ridícula
ni tampoco una burla
no sé en qué creer
ni tampoco qué hacer
sé que no debería temer
pero no sé cómo terminarlo
mientras tanto así seguiré
hasta que aprenda a controlarlo
solo espero con anhelo
el día en que al final
se acabe esta pesadilla
y suelte esta ansiedad

María Magallón is a sophomore at La Joya Early College High School, and among her many hobbies, she enjoys listening to music from which she gets a lot of inspiration to write. She finds it fun and comforting to express and display her feelings and thoughts through writing.

Anxiety

by María Magallón

I look for the exit
Of this dark place
I look for the answers
Of these questions that I carry
What is the matter with you?
Why so much fear?
Are you perhaps a coward?
Or why so much dread?
I am so exhausted
Of not being able to speak
Of not being able to do anything
Without feeling anxiety
I don't want to be ridiculous
Not even a mockery
I don't know what to believe
Nor what to do
I know I shouldn't fear
But I don't know how to end it
In the meantime like this I'll continue
Until I learn how to control it
I just look forward
To the day that in the end
This nightmare is finally over
And I let go of this anxiety

María Magallón is a sophomore at La Joya Early College High School, and among her many hobbies, she enjoys listening to music from which she gets a lot of inspiration to write. She finds it fun and comforting to express and display her feelings and thoughts through writing.

Flower

by Victoria Salinas

Like a seed
Enclosed and grounded, watching
Everyone around growing
And filling the skies with
Beautiful colors galore

Hoping that one day
You too, could blossom
Beautifully

Muddy days
Overwhelming feelings
Longer days
Growing truly is time consuming
Yet, you continue to rise
With strength and green
Some envy such thing

Here you are In full bloom
What felt like eternity
Was worth the wait

In full bloom
Here you are
Painting the skies with your
Beautiful colors

Victoria Salinas is a 11th grader and is currently attending La Joya Early College High School. Victoria in her free time likes to bake and cook. She likes to write about emotions and adventures.

Flor

por Victoria Salinas

Como una semilla
Cerrada y conectada a tierra, mirando
A todos alrededor creciendo
Y llenando los cielos con
Hermosos colores en abundancia

Esperando que un día
Tú también pudieras florecer
Hermosamente

Días fangosos
Sentimientos abrumadores
Días más largos
Crecer realmente lleva mucho tiempo
Sin embargo, sigues subiendo
Con fuerza y verde
Algunos envidian tal cosa

Aquí estás
Floreciente
Lo que se sintió como la eternidad
Valió la pena la espera

Floreciente
Aquí estás
Pintando los cielos
Con tus colores bonitos

Victoria Salinas is a 11th grader and is currently attending La Joya Early College High School. Victoria in her free time likes to bake and cook. She likes to write about emotions and adventures.

Hermano

por Leo Hinojosa

El es trabajador, cuidadoso, tranquilo, tímido
hijo de sus padres orgullosos
Alguien que le encanta el fútbol
Alguien que tiene miedo de perder a un ser amado
es alguien que ama a sus padres y familia
sueña de sus bisabuelos todo los días
Planea estudiar e ir al colegio
Desea trabajar duro para mantener a su familia Trata de ser respetuoso y
cuidadoso
Siempre se pregunta si es una buena persona
Desea ir a visitar a su abuela y abuelo
Se siente feliz y agradecido.
Es una persona que se preocupa por otros.
Desea que sus padres se sientan orgullosos de él.
Este es verdaderamente mi hermano

Leo Hinojosa is a 10th grader and is currently attending La Joya Early College High School. Leo in his free time likes to play Basketball, spend time with his loved ones, and read books. He likes to write about his family, his life and what kind of person he is.

Adarius Wise, 17 years old

De adentro hacia afuera

por José Villanueva

Una sonrisa Motivación clara
Inspiración en todas partes
Ninguna pelea en vista
Disfrutando su tiempo
Viviendo sin arrepentimiento
Una emoción buena y clara
El honor de ser "el hombre"
El guía de vida es claro
La dirección es dada
Por fuera
Su ser querido se fue
La inspiración misma se fue
Su motivación se fue
La pelea fue perdida
Su tiempo se sigue gastando
Los arrepentimientos pesan y duelen
Las emociones mixtas y confusas
La carga de ser "el hombre"
Su guía desaparecido
La dirección perdida Por dentro

José Villanueva is a sophomore at La Joya Early College. He was born on March 30, 2006. José has 3 sisters and his Mother. José spends his time doing many things including, but not limited to, drawing, painting, and origami.

Inside Out

by José Villanueva

A smile
Clear motivation
Inspiration everywhere
No fight in sight
Enjoying their time
Living without regrets
A good and clear emotion
The honor of being "the man"
Life's guide is clear
The direction is given
On the Outside
His loved one is gone
Inspiration itself is gone
Your motivation is gone
The fight was lost
His time is still wasting
Regrets weigh and hurt
Mixed and confused emotions
The burden of being "the man"
Life's guide disappeared
The lost direction
On the Inside

José Villanueva is a sophomore at La Joya Early College. He was born on March 30, 2006. José has 3 sisters and his Mother. José spends his time doing many things including, but not limited to, drawing, painting, and origami.

The Beauty in Kids
by Leslie Martínez

She sees the beauty in kids,
the one no one else can.
The one the world hid,
But she has a plan
To uncover this beauty.

She will prove to the world
the knowledge they have.
The children will be known
for their joy and cheer.
She will do this for the cuties

She knows they are
The future generation
She believes they are
The generation that will
"Make a Change"

She sees the beauty in kids
The one no one else can
And she will never stop
Till they do!!

Leslie Martínez is a 10th grader and is currently attending La Joya Early College High School. Leslie in her free time likes to play with her dogs and to bake. She likes to write about her feelings and how she can be a better person.

"Colorful World"

Fouad Reda
December 13, 2021

Fouad Reda, age 9

Christmas
by Humberto Loredo

bright lights
in all the city
the holidays arrived

todos comiendo turrones
regalos debajo del árbol
y el día ya sin sol

all families prepare
on this very special day
parties everywhere
the children opening their gifts

estoy muy alegre
mientras juego con todos en la nieve
todos cantando canciones navideñas

how much wisdom this day teaches us
you have more to enjoy
a day full of happiness

Humberto is a 10th grader and is currently attending La Joya Early College High School. Humberto in his free time likes to write about special holidays and festivals.

Mother nature
by Kailey Cedillo

Everywhere I go
nature is all around me
Sand beneath my feet or
the water crashing on shore
Beautiful trees everywhere
as well as lovely flower fields

Rocky mountains uniquely formed
and wildlife roaming free
I hear the chirping of the birds,
the croaking of the frogs,
along with the buzzing of the bee's

When there is a thunderstorm
don't be afraid because
a beautiful light show is what we'll see

So much to explore
with so much to see
Mother nature is beautiful
Don't you agree?

Kailey Cedillo is a 10th grader and is currently attending La Joya Early College High School. Kailey in her free time likes to play on her school's volleyball team and enjoys singing. She likes to write about the beautiful world around her and nature.

Mentality
by Humberto García

I used to be scared
Until I figured my weakness

    Mentality

Mentality is a huge personality
Mentality will make you
or break you

It's a personality
Not a characteristic
It could be fixed
No need to trip
Once it's fixed
You will feel mixed

But don't worry
It's all part of the trick

Humberto is a 9th grader and is currently attending La Joya Early College High School. Humberto in his free time likes to play basketball after school with friends. He likes to write about his dreams of becoming a basketball player and his future.

The art of change
by Yuliana Flores

Something good
Something new
Not boring
Without being afraid
Remarkable, isn't it?
How we grow
From caterpillar to butterfly
Wings so beautiful
They can become art
Accepting the new
Because it's something that not everyone has
Why do you do it?
Do you not like it anymore?
Feeling that you need to change
Because it's the only thing
That makes you feel better

Yuliana Flores is an 11th grader and is currently attending La Joya Early College High School. Yuliana in her free time likes to paint, draw, sing, play the guitar, do crossword puzzles, and loves taking pictures of nature. She also likes to read poems that relate to her.

Norma Judith Tavares Rodríguez, age 12

COVID-19

por Nelly Moreno

Una enfermedad que vino desde China
y afectó a todo el mundo
las personas asustadas y preocupadas
de qué iba a suceder con este nuevo virus
avanzó y causó demasiadas muertes

niños y adultos morían cada día
hospitales llenos y desesperados por atender a cada uno de sus pacientes
el CDC quiso hacer algo sobre este virus
CDC obligó a las personas a usar mascarillas y desinfectante
y hasta la frontera tuvo que cerrar

las personas entraron en pánico y se acabaron el papel de baño
CDC puso una orden de restricción
solo dos personas de mayoría de edad podían salir si era una emergencia
y no podían salir después de las doce de la noche

CDC decidió hacer vacunas para este virus
estas vacunas ayudan a prevenir el COVID-19
hicieron para adultos y jóvenes
ahora hasta hay para niños de cinco
hasta doce años
este virus todavía está presente en la humanidad

Nelly Moreno is a 10th grader and is currently attending La Joya Early College High School. Nelly Moreno in her free time likes to do exercise, she likes to write about unforgettable experiences in her life.

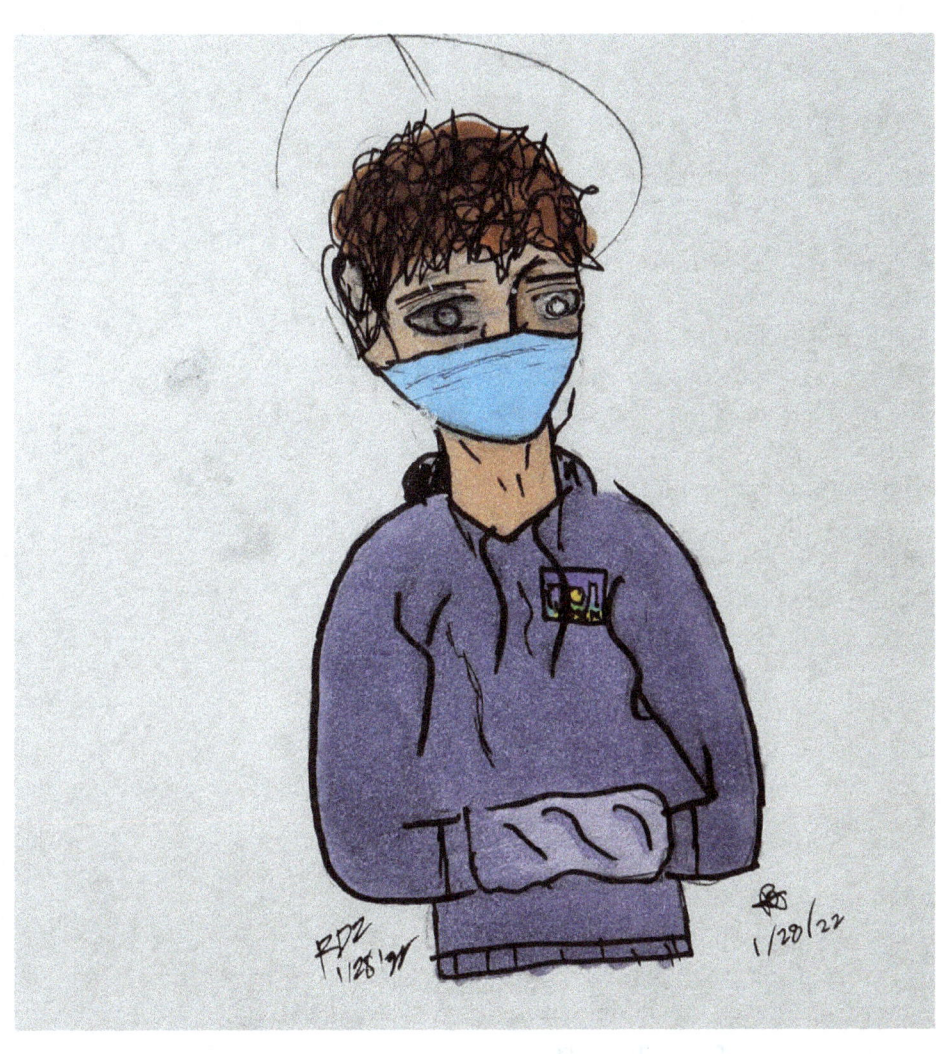

Miguel H. Rodriguez, 13 years old

COVID-19

by Nelly Moreno

A disease that came from China and
affected the world
Frightened and worried people
What was going to happen with this new virus
The virus advanced too far that there were too many deaths

Children and even adults died every day
Hospitals full and desperate to care for each of their patients
The CDC wanted to do something about this virus.
CDC forced people to wear masks and disinfectant
And even the border had to close

People panicked and ran out of toilet paper
CDC placed a restraining order
Only two people of legal age could leave if it was an emergency.
And they couldn't leave after twelve o'clock at night.

CDC decided to make vaccines for this virus
These vaccines help prevent the spread of COVID-19
That were made for adults and the youth
Now there are even for children from five to twelve years old
This virus is still present in humanity

Nelly Moreno is a 10th grader and is currently attending La Joya Early College High School. Nelly Moreno in her free time likes to do exercise, she likes to write about unforgettable experiences in her life.

Growing Up
by Kendra García

As young
as I am
I fear
getting old
I fear death
The thoughts sink deeply into my head
I want to be young forever
The thought of being old
is horrifying
Getting sick
Being in pain
Is what comes along
with growing up
It's what I fear most
growing up

Kendra García is a 9th grader and is currently attending La Joya Early College High School. Kendra in her free time likes to dance with her high school drill team. She likes to write about her fears.

Why him
by Angelina Muñoz

You smell like roses
If only you could see
How much you mean to me

But you'll leave me for him
I don't like him
I hate him

Why couldn't you love me instead
It should've been me
Not him

He doesn't deserve you
You're too lovely
I've always been better

I'm the one you should be with
Not him
Me

Angelina Muñoz is a 9th grader and is currently attending La Joya Early College High School. Angelina Muñoz in her free time likes to read or draw.

Life

by Catherine Rosas

Life is beautiful
It is like a movie
It is full of beautiful moments
It can be very cruel with the best people
It can also have its bad moments

Life is short

We must try to enjoy it all
We will meet special people
Also people who love us to make people suffer
And with the people we love,

Life is joyful

Never goes as planned
It is full of surprises
And in life, everything has a reason

Life is like a bike,
so as not to fall, you need to move on

Catherine Rosas is a tenth grader and is currently attending La Joya Early College High School.Catherine in her free time likes to play soccer. She likes to write about life.

Elyse Castillo - age 15

Estoy tan cansada
por Azeneth Orduña

Estoy tan cansada
Pero no de mi cuerpo
Duermo y como bien
Pero mi mente está tan cansada
Y no entiendo el porqué
Soy joven y me falta mucho
por ver y lograr
¿Pero cómo lo logró?
A ciegas sigo con el ritmo cotidiano
¿Pero cuál es mi inspiración?
¿Qué me puede ayudar a descansar mi mente?
¿Qué me puede dar la inspiración y la energía?
Que yo tanto anhelo
Estoy tan cansada
Y ya no lo quiero estar
Quiero solo un descanso
Para poder continuar...

I'm so tired
by Azeneth Orduña

I'm so tired
But not from my body
I sleep and eat well
But my mind is so tired
I don't understand why
I'm young and there is still so much
to see and achieve
But how can I achieve it?
Blindly I go with the daily rhythm
But what is my inspiration?
Who can help me rest my mind?
What can give me inspiration and energy?
That I so much crave
I'm so tired
And I don't want to be so anymore
I only want to rest
So that I can continue...

Azeneth Orduña is in the tenth grade and is currently attending La Joya Early College High School. She enjoys the simple things of life such as playing with her pets and going out with family.

NEVER GIVE UP

by Angelyn Gutiérrez

If you ever feel like giving up
Don't
If it ever looks like you're not
Going to make it
Keep going
There's no excuses for giving up
You only live once
Live life like if there's no tomorrow
No matter what you're facing always remember
Life is beautiful just the way it is
We've got to fail in order to succeed in life
And even if it's hard
And we may struggle
Never give up, pick yourself up
And continue fighting...

Angelyn Gutiérrez is a 9th grader and is currently attending La Joya Early College High School. Angelyn Gutiérrez in her free time likes to play with her dog. She likes to write about her personal life.

Stressed

by Carolina Sepúlveda

Stressed out, stressed out
Everyday something new
Thinking of what to do
Should I just stop whatever I'm doing?
Do I keep going forward?
Running my hands through my hair
I realize that stress is getting to me
Procrastinating, procrastinating
Something I frequently do
Stressing myself out
Worrying if I'm ever going to stop
Thinking of what to do
My hands start to get sweaty
Everyday gets harder
Stressed out, stressed out

Carolina Sepúlveda is a ninth grader and is currently attending La Joya Early College High School. In her free time, she likes to spend lots of time with her family and enjoy every moment of it. Carolina likes to mainly write about her feelings and her thoughts about her life.

Madura

por Madeleine Poiree

Siempre me he sentido mayor de lo que soy.
toda mi vida he sido madura
estaba montada arriba de una ola de expectativas
no preparada para la caída

uno solo puede viajar tan alto por tanto tiempo
antes de llegar a un punto muerto,
una pausa.
es una cosa peculiar
ser buena para tu edad
porque todos llegamos a un momento

dónde paramos de ser buenos
dónde crecemos más allá de nuestra fecha de expiración
dónde nos hundimos en el océano, nuestras alas de cera disolviéndose

O como Ícaro, volando hasta que nos quemamos y cayendo de todos modos.
soy una niña.
soy joven y fuerte y despistada.
pero siempre me he sentido mayor de lo que soy.

Madeleine Poiree is a 16- year old La Joya Early College High school student. She has always loved reading and found comfort in writing, whether it be stories or poems, from a very young age.

La vida no es lo que parece

por Karina Ascencio

No todo se trata de felicidad
Vienen días malos
Días tristes a continuación
La vida no es fácil
Difícil de encontrar trabajos
Pagar facturas no es fácil
Estrés,
Falla,
No todo te será dado
Pero trabajar duro puede llevarte a cualquier parte
Habrá altibajos
Habrá tiempos difíciles
Pero todo vale la pena
Tal vez no hoy
Tal vez no mañana
Pero lo será en el futuro

Karina Ascencio is a 10th grader and is currently attending La Joya Early College High School. Karina Ascencio in her free time likes to dance folklórico and read while listening to music.

Sofia Linn is 11 years old

Life is not what it seems
by Karina Ascencio

Not everything is about happiness
Bad days come,
Sad days next
Life is not easy
Hard to find jobs
Paying bills isnt easy
Stress,
Failure,
Not everything will be given to you
But working hard can get you anywhere
There will be ups and downs
There will be hard times
But everything is worth it
Maybe not today
Maybe not tomorrow
But it will in the future

Karina Ascencio is a 10th grader and is currently attending La Joya Early College High School. Karina Ascencio in her free time likes to dance folklórico and read while listening to music.

Sad, Cold Days

by Arlette Hernández

A springtime, however hard it tries
Will always be stormy.
Does springtime make you shiver?
I saw the cold season of my generation destroyed,
How I mourned the wintertime.
Wintertime is refrigerated. Wintertime is inhuman,
Wintertime is glacial, however.
When I think of the summer, I see a mild model.
Does summer make you shiver?
Does it?
Just like cold days,
"Shuffle", said the winter,
& "shuffle" & "shuffle" again.

Arlette Hernández is a 9th grader and is currently attending La Joya
Early Colleage High School. Arlette Hernández during her free time likes
to play softball and she likes to write about scary stories.

Scary Winter

by Arlette Hernández

Dark days
Snow falling
Humidity in the air
Sticky air
People dying
Diseases spreading
Lonely kids
Not being loved
Died

Arlette Hernández is a 9th grader and is currently attending La Joya Early College High School. Arlette Hernández during her free time likes to play softball and she likes to write about scary stories.

La joven hambrienta y su amante
por Kimberly Vela

Había una vez una niña
Una joven hambrienta

Sus ojos siempre estaban enfocados en el mundo sucio
Mientras su espalda miraba hacia el paraíso limpio
Su boca formaba gritos cuando llegaba el viento
El viento frío rasgando su piel
Pero su amante
Ocupado escribiendo una melodía
Vino a rescatarla de abajo

Pero luego, más tarde, no se le permitió mirar atrás
Para mirar atrás y enfrentar a su propio amante mientras caminaba
Porque pensaba que los seres de abajo lo engañaban
Pero pronto se olvidó de que tal cosa

Una cosa simple
Terminaría en tragedia

Kimberly Vela is a 11th grader and is currently attending La Joya Early College High School. Kimberly in her free time likes to sing and draw. She likes to write about tragedy and romance.

That Day
by Jéssica López

It all happened that day…
I stood there, shocked to my core
Not knowing what to do
What to think
I felt as if there wasn't enough air
My knees were ready to give
I could barely stand
I felt fraile
I fell…
Fell straight to my knees
I felt stuck. I couldn't move.
My mothers voice echoed above me

She picked me up
Gave me a warm embrace
I stayed frozen
I felt stuck. I couldn't move.

She comforted me
Said "Everything will be ok"
I believed her…because
People can't feel stuck forever

Jéssica López is currently a 9th grader at La Joya Early College High School. In Jessica's free time she likes to spend time with her family and friends. She likes to write about topics that are important to her and topics she thinks other people will find interesting.

Moon

by Génesis Gracia

I look up to you when night is upon us.
Sometimes you're full
Sometimes you're a half
And occasionally a quarter
No matter the size you're always there
You are the moon I always stare . .
Sometimes I can barely see you
Sometimes you are a different color
But no matter how you look like
Or what color you are
I always know you're there
Your presence warms my heart
And provides me peace
Thanks to you I can sleep
I love the way you can shine so bright
And provide me the most beautiful light
Through the night you're all I see
And I wouldn't' have it any other way

Génesis Gracia is a 9th grader and is currently attending La Joya Early College HS. Génesis Gracia in her free time likes to play basketball with her friends and go out to eat with her beautiful family. She likes to write about lessons she has learned through the past years.

Kreideprinz

by Kathlyn Duberney

Built by the hands of gold
Two brothers made of chalk
Together from a nation that gods feared

The first failed
Imprisoned forever in a
flying beast's heart
Never to be seen again
The second was successful
A reclusive genius blessed by the Lord of Geo
Studying far above in the mountains
Where the snow never seems to melt
What was once a creation has become the creator
A golden mark surrounded by pale skin
Proof he is adored by the stars
Two brothers reunited once again
The first filled with jealousy for the second
Impersonating him til there's only one
Two brothers alike and yet different
Two halves of the same coin
Now, dear traveler, can you tell whose
The second brother?

Kathlyn Duberney is a 11th grader and is currently attending La Joya Early College High School. Kathlyn in his free time likes to create small nick nacks. They like to write about anything she finds interesting. Previously published in *Boundless 2020*.

The Noise

by Samantha Caballero

What is that noise?
She hears it everywhere
She hears it in the morning
She hears it at midnight
She hears it in her dreams
She hears it when she eats
She hears it when she sleeps
She hears it when she does chores
She hears it when she does work
Is it a mouse?
Is it a water leak?
Is it a pipe?
Is it a mother just doing her chores?
It makes her wonder
What is that noise?

Samantha Caballero is a 10th grader and is currently attending La Joya Early College High School. Samantha Caballero in her free time likes to draw and write about other artists.

Family

by Paola Fernández

What would life be without having people you call family?
When your world is falling apart, who would be there to support you?
Family is more than just a simple six letter word
Family is the strength needed to overcome challenges
The light at the end of the tunnel
Family is unbreakable
A bond that is forever
A blessing like no other
A shoulder you need to cry on
A helping hand in tough situations
The unconditional love handed down generation to generation
Keeps growing stronger along the way
They may not be always be by blood
But it is the people who you can trust and will never leave your side
This is the true meaning of family

Paola Fernández is a 10th grader and is currently attending La Joya Early College High School. Paola Fernández in her free time likes to dance, read books, spend time with her family, and go out with friends. She likes to write about what she loves and is passionate about.

VIPF 2022 EVENTS

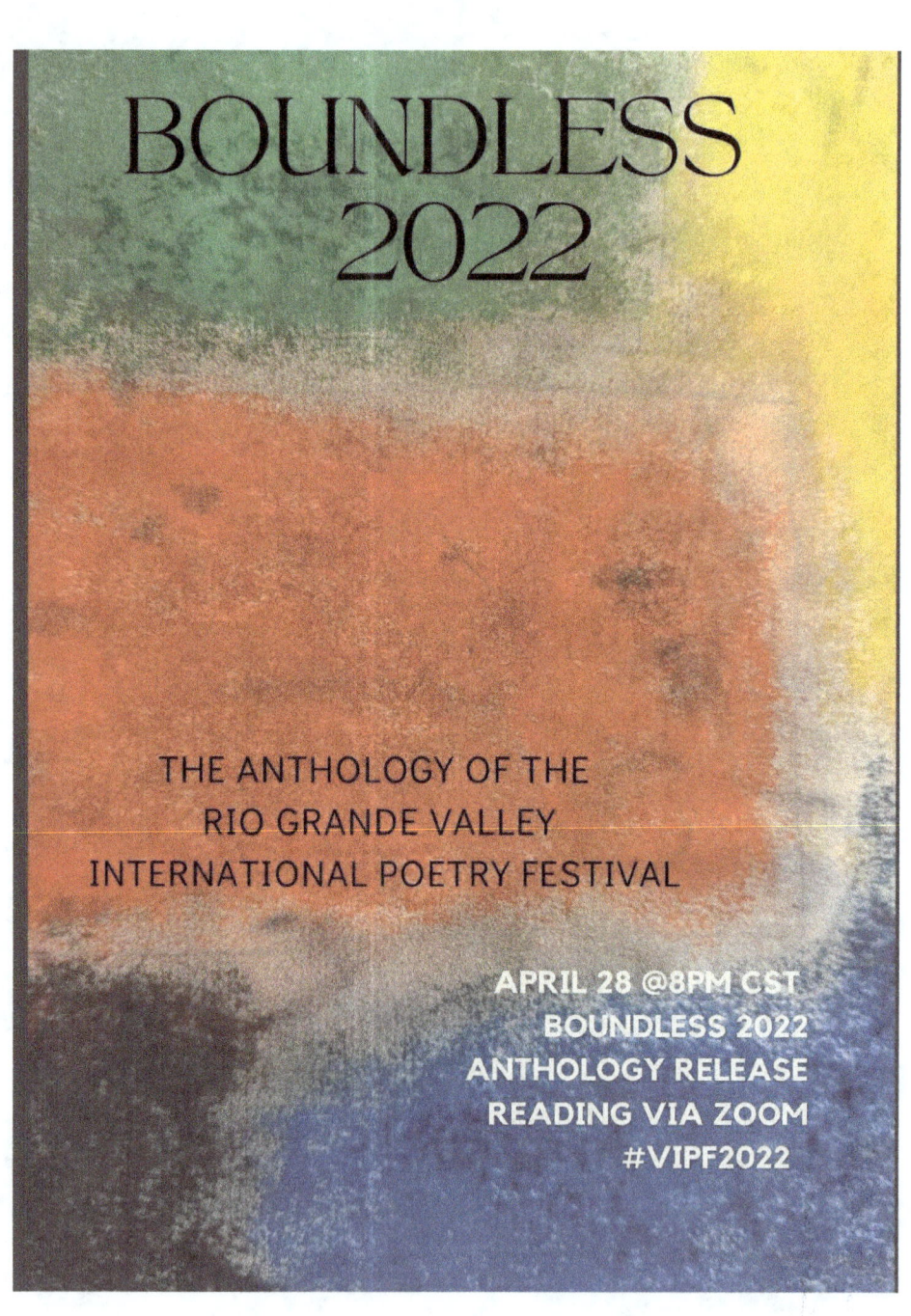

BOUNDLESS
2022

THE ANTHOLOGY OF THE
RIO GRANDE VALLEY
INTERNATIONAL POETRY FESTIVAL

APRIL 28 @8PM CST
BOUNDLESS 2022
ANTHOLOGY RELEASE
READING VIA ZOOM
#VIPF2022

**Viernes
29 de
abril a las
18:30 h.**

**UN EVENTO
VIRTUAL VIPF
VOZ ESENCIAL:
ESPECIAL VIPF
EDICIÓN EN
ESPAÑOL**

VALLEYPOETRYFEST.ORG

15TH ANNUAL

V.I.P.F.

Presentando:
Paula Abramo,
Liliana Valenzuela,
Balam Rodrigo,
Benito Pastoriza
Iyodo, & Gabriel
González Núñez

DECOLONIZING OUR WRITING

SATURDAY, APRIL 30 @ 11 A.M.
- Stories and Poetry of Witness, Recounting, and Resistance
- A Generative Workshop with Odilia Galván Rodríguez

ODILIA GALVÁN RODRÍGUEZ

15TH ANNUAL
V.I.P.F.
RIO GRANDE VALLEY
INTERNATIONAL POETRY FESTIVAL
WWW.VALLEYPOETRYFEST.ORG

In this workshop, through free writing, we will explore ways to reincorporate our ways of speaking, telling stories, code-switching, and writing in the languages of our ancestors. We may have lost some of our indigenous languages; however, we may begin to remember them by writing freely without worrying about the audience or the gatekeepers. Register Webinar ID 816 9803 5614
#VIPF2022

valleypoetryfest.org

238

ARIANA

A READING AND Q&A

BROWN

15TH ANNUAL

V.I.P.F.

RIO GRANDE VALLEY
INTERNATIONAL POETRY FESTIVAL
WWW.VALLEYPOETRYFEST.ORG

VALLEYPOETRYFEST.ORG

This special reading
and Q&A with author
ARIANA BROWN are
in community with
UTRGV, MAS, The
Center for Diversity
and Inclusion and
DREAM Resource
Center

- Saturday, April 30 @ 2:15 p.m.

- Nadie escuchó tu llanto/No One Heard Your Cries

- Presented by featured poet Xánath Caraza

#vipf2022

SATURDAY, APRIL 30 @ 3:30 P.M.

I Once Was Lost, but Now I... Found Poetry: Examining Six Ways to Cut Up and Mix Poems Presented by Mark Esperanza #vipf2022

www.vallepoetryfest.org

valleypoetryfest.org

30th April, 2022

Publishing
Workshop

We will focus in this class on key aspects of editing, research, community, submitting, rejection, and staying focused. Please be prepared with writing materials. **#VIPF2022**

Edward Vidaurre

15TH ANNUAL

V.I.P.F.

RIO GRANDE VALLEY
INTERNATIONAL POETRY FESTIVAL
WWW.VALLEYPOETRYFEST.ORG

POETRY IN MOTION –
CHALLENGING THE BOUNDARIES
OF POETRY AND PLAYWRITING

Gerry Rodriguez

SUNDAY, MAY 1 @ 12PM
POETRY IN MOTION –
CHALLENGING THE
BOUNDARIES OF POETRY
AND PLAYWRITING

Gerry Rodriguez is a
candidate in the MFA
Creative Writing program at
University of Texas Rio
Grande Valley where she
studies playwriting and
poetry.

Rio Grande Valley International Poetry Festival #VIPF2022

Sunday, May 1 @ 2:15 pm
I Sing: The Body
anthology presentation

RENÉ SALDAÑA, JR. (PRESENTING)
May 1, 2022 @ 2:15 PM CST
Virtual Reading

Emotional trauma and isolation during the pandemic has had devastaPoems about Body Image an anthology Presented by René Saldaña, Jr.ting and lasting effects on our mental and physical health. Friends and family report stress, anxiety, doubt, uncertainty, and fear in these unparalleled times.

I SING : THE BODY
Poems about Body Image

15TH ANNUAL
V.I.P.F.
RIO GRANDE VALLEY
INTERNATIONAL POETRY FESTIVAL
WWW.VALLEYPOETRYFEST.ORG

edited by René Saldaña, Jr.

DAVID ROMERO

MODERATES

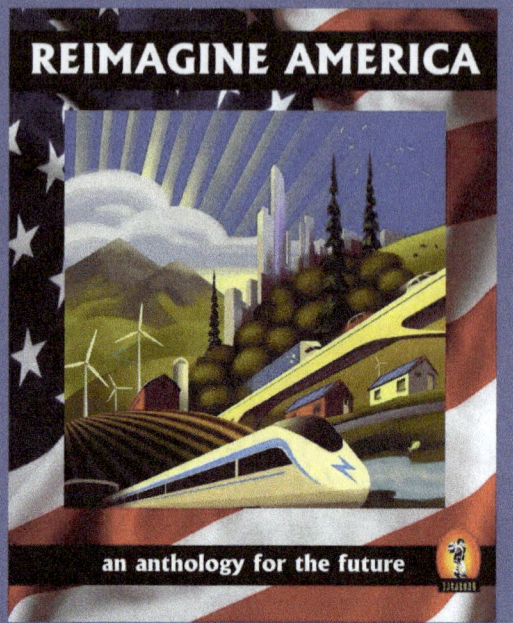

A Presentation of
REIMAGINE AMERICA: an anthology for the future
from Vagabond Books

JOAN LANGE - MATT SEDILLO -
MAHNAZ BADIHIAN - MEGHA SOOD
DAVID DEPHY - TREVA "HISPOET" JOHNSON
DEE ALLEN - AIYANA SHA'NIEL -
ELIZABETH MARINO

Sunday, May 1 @ 3:15 pm via zoom
#VIPF2022

SUNDAY, MAY 1
@ 7PM

VIPF PRESENTS

FLOWERSONG PRESS
AUTHOR SHOWCASE

PRESENTED BY
EDWARD VIDAURRE

MATT SEDILLO - DANIEL GARCÍA ORDAZ -
KAI COGGIN - TATIANA FIGUEROA RAMIREZ
KRISTINE ESSER SLENTZ - REBECCA BOWMAN
EDDIE VEGA - AYEYEMI TAOFEEK - MEGHA SOOD
TOM MURPHY - FERNANDO ALBERT SALINAS
KAMALA PLATT - GINA DURAN -IRIS DE ANDA
CÉSAR L. DE LEÓN - LUIVETTE RESTO -
LETICIA URIETA - STEVEN ALVAREZ-
RAÚL SÁNCHEZ - R. JOSEPH RODRÍGUEZ -
MARISOL CORTEZ - ODILIA GALVÁN RODRÍGUEZ
REBECCA BOWMAN

#VIPF2022